Relating to Others in Love

A Study of Romans 12–16

Bible Study Guide

From the Bible-teaching ministry of

Charles R. Swindoll

Published by

INSIGHT FOR LIVING

Post Office Box 4444
Fullerton, California 92634

Distributed by

Educational Products Division
Waco, Texas 76796

This guide is the third in a series of three study guides on the Book of Romans. These studies are based on the outlines of sermons delivered by Charles R. Swindoll. Chuck is a graduate of Dallas Theological Seminary and has served in pastorates for over twenty-two years, including churches in Texas, New England, and California. Since 1971 he has served as senior pastor of the First Evangelical Free Church of Fullerton, California. Chuck's radio program, "Insight for Living," began in 1979. In addition to his church and radio ministries, Chuck has authored twenty books and numerous booklets on a variety of subjects.

Chuck's outlines are expanded from the sermon transcripts and edited by Bill Watkins, a graduate of California State University at Fresno and Dallas Theological Seminary, with the assistance of Bill Butterworth, a graduate of Florida Bible College, Dallas Theological Seminary, and Florida Atlantic University. Bill Watkins is presently the director of educational resources, and Bill Butterworth is currently the director of counseling ministries at Insight for Living.

Publisher: Insight for Living, Fullerton, California
Creative Director: Cynthia Swindoll
Editor: Bill Watkins
Associate Editor: Bill Butterworth
Editorial Assistants: Rebecca Anderson, Jane Gillis, Wendy Jones, Julie Martin, and Karene Wells

Communications Manager: Carla Beck
Production Supervisor: Deedee Snyder
Production Assistant: Linda Robertson
Production Artists: Trina Crockett, Rhonda DiBello, Donna Mayo, and Jim Wikle

Typographer: Trina Crockett
Calligrapher: Richard Stumpf
Cover Designer: Michael Standlee
Printer: R. R. Donnelley & Sons Co.
Cover: Painting by Myles Birket Foster, *The Swing,* reproduced by courtesy of the Medici Society, London, England; Graphic Arts Unlimited, Inc.

An album that contains sixteen messages on eight cassettes and corresponds to this study guide may be purchased through Insight for Living, Post Office Box 4444, Fullerton, California 92634. For information, please write for the current Insight for Living catalog, or call (714) 870-9161. Canadian residents may direct their correspondence to Insight for Living Ministries, Post Office Box 2510, Vancouver, British Columbia, Canada V6B 3W7, or call (604) 669-1916.

ISBN 0-8499-8216-2

Table of Contents

Relating to Others in Love

The value of Romans is legendary. Down through the centuries Christians have turned to this letter perhaps more often than any other in the New Testament. It gives our faith backbone. It strengthens our confidence in God. It clarifies our understanding of the salvation we have received. It lifts our sights above the petty irritations of life on earth and reminds us of our sure hope in the Lord Jesus Christ.

But that only covers the first eleven chapters! When we arrive at the twelfth chapter—one of the greatest in all of Scripture—we begin to bring into proper focus our relationship with others . . . others inside the family as well as outside of the family. And instead of the emphasis falling on doctrinal faith and heavenly hope, the theme changes to authentic love—a needed emphasis!

I am pleased to continue traveling with you along the Romans' road. This section is exceedingly practical—my kind of teaching! So let's be open and ready to hear what God's Spirit has to say about relating to others in love.

Chuck Swindoll

Chuck Swindoll

Putting Truth into Action

Knowledge apart from application falls short of God's desire for His children. Knowledge must result in change and growth. Consequently, we have constructed this Bible study guide with these purposes in mind: (1) to stimulate discovery, (2) to increase understanding, and (3) to encourage application.

At the end of each lesson is a section called ***Living Insights.*** *There you'll be given assistance in further Bible study, thoughtful interaction, and personal appropriation. This is the place where the lesson is fitted with shoe leather for your walk through the varied experiences of life.*

In wrapping up some lessons, you'll find a unit called  ***Digging Deeper.*** *It will provide you with essential information and list helpful resource materials so that you can probe further into some of the issues raised in those studies.*

It's our hope that you'll discover numerous ways to use this tool. Some useful avenues we would suggest are personal meditation, joint discovery, and discussion with your spouse, family, work associates, friends, or neighbors. The study guide is also practical for church classes, and, of course, as a study aid for the "Insight for Living" radio broadcast. The individual studies can usually be completed in thirty minutes. However, some are more open-ended and could be expanded for greater depth. Their use is flexible!

In order to derive the greatest benefit from this process, we suggest that you record your responses to the lessons in a notebook where writing space is plentiful. In view of the kinds of questions asked, your notebook may become a journal filled with your many discoveries and commitments. We anticipate you will find yourself returning to it periodically for review and encouragement.

Bill Watkins
Editor

Bill Butterworth
Associate Editor

Relating to Others in Love

A Study of Romans 12–16

How Faith Functions

Romans 12:1–8

Throughout the first eleven chapters of Romans, the Apostle Paul lays down these foundational truths of the gospel—sin, justification, sanctification, glorification, and sovereignty. In the final chapters of this epistle, Paul sets his sights on *service*. He provides us with divinely inspired guidelines for applying the Christian faith. If we want God to use us to our full potential, then we need to pay close attention to what these verses teach. So let's get out our walking shoes and prepare for the journey. We are about to learn how God wants us to relate to others in love.

I. Looking Within (Romans 12:1–3).

Speaking to Christians, Paul specifies three phases of dedication to God. Each one is essential to the outworking of vibrant Christianity in life.

A. Consecration (v. 1). Paul opens chapter 12 with an urgent plea, which functions as the third major conclusion in the book (see Rom. 5:1 and 8:1). Notice his exhortation: "I urge you therefore, brethren, by the mercies of God, to present your bodies a living and holy sacrifice, acceptable to God, which is your spiritual [literally, rational] service of worship" (Rom. 12:1). This passage calls on believers to consecrate themselves to God. Christians should willfully reserve the totality of their lives for the Lord's good purposes. However, because believers are live rather than dead sacrifices, they have a tendency to want to crawl off the altar. That's why this deliberate decision to place oneself at God's disposal must be made repeatedly, not once and for all.

B. Transformation (v. 2). In this verse Paul gives believers two commands. The first one is, "Do not be conformed to this world." The word *conformed* means "to assume an outward expression that does not come from within." When we conform ourselves to the world's anti-God mold, we externally exhibit characteristics that fail to reflect our new life in Christ. Put another way, we begin to image non-Christian values and concerns rather than Christian ones. Therefore, Paul calls on us to stop mimicking the world's system and start becoming "transformed by the renewing" of our minds. The term *transformed* means "to assume an outward expression that reflects what is deep within." We are told to continue allowing our external lifestyle to match our internal, saved condition. The key to this process is our minds, for it is our thought life that controls our attitudes, feelings, and actions. In other words, we are to let our lives be altered from the inside out. The Holy Spirit accomplishes this transformation process by reshaping our thinking. The end result of His work and our submission to it is our conformity to the Lord's perfect will—namely, the renewal of each of us into the image of God's Son (Rom. 8:29, 12:2; 2 Cor. 3:18; Col. 3:10–11).

C. Evaluation (v. 3). The role we are to play in the transformation process includes proper self-evaluation. Paul counsels us as to how we can think correctly about ourselves. His first piece of instruction is negative: "I say to every man among you not to think more highly of himself than he ought to think." We are not to be prideful or conceited in our self-assessment. On the positive side, however, Paul tells us "to think so as to have sound judgment, as God has allotted to each a measure of faith." We need to gain an accurate, honest view of ourselves. This process encompasses coming to a realistic conclusion about our strengths and weaknesses, God-given talents and human deficiencies. In short, we are not to view ourselves as either all-important or totally insignificant. Rather, we are exhorted to have an accurate appraisal of ourselves and to be satisfied with our place in God's program.

II. Serving Others (Romans 12:4–8).

Consecration, transformation, and evaluation are prerequisites to Christian service. But once we have looked within ourselves and have correctly assessed where we are, then we are ready to look outside ourselves and seek out where God might want to use us. With this in mind, Paul turns the spotlight on the church and reveals how believers can minister within it.

A. The Body of Christ (vv. 4–5). In these verses Paul compares the church with the human body: "For just as we have many members in one body and all the members do not have the same function, so we, who are many, are one body in Christ, and individually members one of another." Conveyed through these words are two essential truths about the Church universal as well as each local assembly. First, *the Church is composed of* *many members.* Just as the various parts of the human body have different yet important functions, so the numerous individuals who comprise the Body of Christ also have unique and vital roles. Second, *the Church's members are interrelated.* The members of the human body are dependent on one another for the proper functioning of the body as a whole. Likewise, the only way for the Body of Christ to experience vitality, health, and balance is by its members working for the benefit of all. Thus, the Church is supposed to be an expression of variety operating in unity.

B. The Believers in the Body (vv. 6–8). The local church experiences growth fostered by unity when believers properly exercise their spiritual gifts. Paul makes three points that are vital to an accurate understanding of this fact. The first one is that *we all have gifts.* No one becomes a believer without also receiving one or more God-given talents. Furthermore, *the gifts we possess differ.* The Lord does not give all of us the same abilities. If He did, then the Body of Christ would be unable to function in a healthy, balanced way. And finally, *we are to exercise our gifts for the benefit of the Body.* Paul illustrates this point by referring to seven exemplary gifts: "if prophecy, according to the proportion of his faith; if service, in his serving; or he who teaches, in his teaching; or he who exhorts, in his exhortation; he who gives, with liberality; he who leads, with diligence; he who shows mercy, with cheerfulness" (vv. 6b–8). Once we discover which gifts God has given us, then we know in what areas He expects us to make major contributions. Of course, we are not to serve for the purpose of self-exaltation, but we are to reach out for the purpose of building up others in the faith (cf. 1 Cor. 12:4–7, 25; Eph. 4:11–16; 1 Pet. 4:10–11).

III. Applying the Message.

The counsel in these verses affects us personally and corporately. Indeed, we can best view the application of this instruction by (1) focusing on ourselves and (2) zeroing in on our relationships with other believers.

A. In Relationship to Ourselves. Two principles stand out as we consider our vertical relationship with God and how it affects our horizontal relationships with Christians.

1. **Accepting ourselves precedes giving of ourselves.** Feelings of insignificance and uselessness only paralyze us. We cannot serve others until we get an accurate picture of our worth in Christ.

2. **Giving of ourselves means accepting others for who they are.** No matter what capacity God has given to us for service, it has been designed to be used for building others up, not for tearing them down.

B. **In Relationship to Others.** From this section of Romans, we discover three telltale characteristics of a healthy, local church.

1. **Genuine Spirituality.** A thriving church displays the flow of authentic, Spirit-filled Christianity from its members.
2. **Positive Spontaneity.** The health of a local assembly can be measured by the willingness of its members to get involved in ministry without the continuous prodding of its church leaders.
3. **Life-giving Sacrifice.** A vital community of believers exhibits an unhindered giving of themselves and their gifts without an inappropriate regard to personal costs.

Living Insights

Study One

Romans 12 begins with the familiar words, "I urge you therefore . . ." Whenever we see the term *therefore,* we should always ask, What is it there for? The answer to that question is found in the preceding eleven chapters.

- Let's look back over Romans 1–11. As you conduct your review, jot down important facts found in these chapters. Then think about what significance those truths have in relationship to the exhortations found in the opening verses of Romans 12. You may find the following chart to be a handy tool in organizing your discoveries.

Reviewing Key Points—Romans 1–11	
Facts Worth Remembering	Verses

Living Insights

Study Two

We've titled this study guide *Relating to Others in Love,* which is one of the major themes of Romans 12–16. Let's get an overview of these five chapters in order to see how we should relate to one another.

- After you copy this chart into your notebook, read through Romans 12–16. Ask yourself this question: According to these verses, how should I be relating to others? As answers arise from your study, write them down.

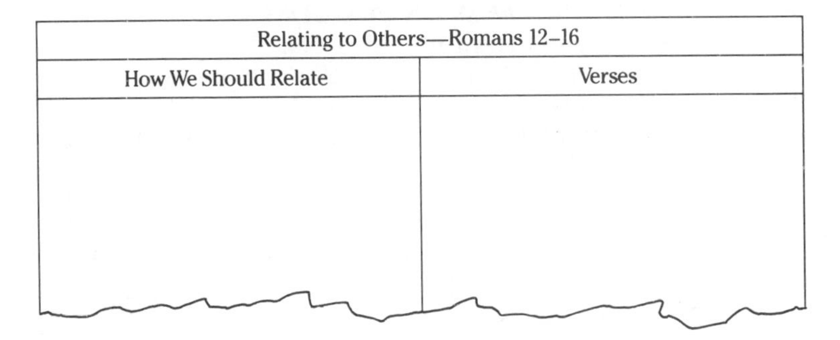

Relating to Others—Romans 12–16	
How We Should Relate	Verses

Digging Deeper

Two matters were raised in this lesson into which you may wish to probe further—*mind renewal* and *spiritual gifts.* The issue of the mind concerns not only the content of our thoughts but also the manner in which we think. There are many philosophies and world views today that clamor for control of our minds either overtly or covertly. But God calls on us to do what Paul and his companions did. Paul explained their activity in these words: "We are destroying speculations and every lofty thing raised up against the knowledge of God, and we are taking every thought captive to the obedience of Christ" (2 Cor. 10:5). The whole subject of spiritual gifts is vital to the healthy functioning of both the local and worldwide church. But many Christians do not know (1) what spiritual gifts are, (2) which ones are available today, or (3) how they can discover which gifts God has given them. So that you might learn more about Christian thinking and spiritual serving, we have listed some of the best sources that deal with these matters. Our hope is that you will use these resources as springboards for further thought and as aids to more effective application.

- **References on Mind Renewal.**

Barclay, Oliver R. *The Intellect and Beyond.* Academie Books. Grand Rapids: Zondervan Publishing House, 1985.

Blamires, Harry. *The Christian Mind: How Should a Christian Think?* Ann Arbor: Servant Books, 1978.

Hoover, A. J. *Don't You Believe It!* Chicago: Moody Press, 1982.

Stott, John R. W. *Your Mind Matters: The Place of the Mind in the Christian Life.* Downers Grove: Inter-Varsity Press, 1972.

Strauss, Richard L. *Win the Battle for Your Mind.* Wheaton: Victor Books, 1980.

Swindoll, Charles R. *Make Up Your Mind . . . about the Issues of Life.* Portland: Multnomah Press, 1981.

Woodbridge, John D., editor. *Renewing Your Mind in a Secular World.* Chicago: Moody Press, 1985.

- **References on Spiritual Gifts.**

Babcox, Neil. *A Search for Charismatic Reality: One Man's Pilgrimage.* Portland: Multnomah Press, 1985.

Baxter, Ronald E. *Gifts of the Spirit.* Grand Rapids: Kregel Publications, 1983.

Edgar, Thomas R. *Miraculous Gifts: Are They for Today?* Neptune: Loizeaux Brothers, 1983.

Marston, George W. *Tongues Then and Now.* Phillipsburg: Presbyterian and Reformed Publishing Co., 1983.

Swindoll, Charles R. *Tongues: An Answer to Charismatic Confusion.* Portland: Multnomah Press, 1981.

Unger, Merrill F. *The Baptism and Gifts of the Holy Spirit.* Chicago: Moody Press, 1974.

Unger, Merrill F. *New Testament Teaching on Tongues.* Grand Rapids: Kregel Publications, 1971.

Walvoord, John F. *The Holy Spirit.* 3d edition. Grand Rapids: Zondervan Publishing House, 1958.

Warfield, B. B. *Counterfeit Miracles.* Reprint edition. Carlisle: The Banner of Truth Trust, 1976.

Yohn, Rick. *Discover Your Spiritual Gift and Use It.* Wheaton: Tyndale House Publishers, Inc., 1974.

Love Exposed

Romans 12:9–13

In another Pauline letter, the superiority of love is exclaimed in this familiar verse: "But now abide faith, hope, love, these three; but the greatest of these is love" (1 Cor. 13:13). Most of us have no trouble believing in the truth of this verse. Neither do we we lack opportunities to demonstrate love to others. So why don't we take advantage of these opportunities? Largely because we choose not to. In the middle section of Romans 12, the Apostle Paul brings us face-to-face with real love. The central point woven throughout the fabric of his words is simply this: *Genuine love is sacrificial involvement in the lives of others.* Any claim to love that is marked by indifference and uninvolvement is not true but false love. Let's get serious about the scriptural teaching on love. The best place to start doing this is in these several verses from Romans 12.

I. Where Love Starts.

Authentic love cannot flow on a horizontal plane until its vertical relationship with God has been established. Among other things, this involves the dedication of ourselves to Him.

A. Before God (Rom. 12:1–2). Love can begin to pour forth from our lives once we place ourselves at God's disposal. This worshipful act of *consecration* will usher in the process of *transformation.* In this phase of dedication to God, our attitudes, feelings, and actions start to change as the Holy Spirit reshapes our mind-set. He turns our focus off the world and on to God. Without this divine work in our lives, we could not begin to love others as we should.

B. Within Ourselves (Rom. 12:3). As we are mentally transformed, we become able to properly *evaluate* ourselves. And in doing so, we learn that we are worthy, purposeful people whom God has gifted in various ways so that we may contribute to the lives of others.

II. When Love Flows.

The proper exercise of our spiritual gifts in the Body of Christ cannot be attained apart from an other-oriented love. Perhaps that's why Paul follows his exhortation about serving through our gifts (vv. 4–8) with directives that concern ministering out of love. Let's take some time to delve into his counsel.

A. Two Major Characteristics of Love (Rom. 12:9). In this verse we find several commands that reveal two key traits of Christian love. The first characteristic of real love is that it is *unhypocritical.* A person who verbally elevates an individual while internally churning with hatred toward that same person is not expressing true love. The love that Christians are to share is an outward expression of what lies deep inside. Honesty that is tempered by humility, grace, and tact is its hallmark. The second trait of authentic love is *discrimination.* This has nothing to do with playing favorites, bigotry, or prejudice. But it does involve abhorring "what is evil" and clinging to "what is good." In other words, genuine love rejects the many faces of evil and stands against them at every turn. Real love bonds itself to all that is good and supports the virtuous in every possible way.

B. Several Accompanying Objectives of Love (Rom. 12:10–13). Now that we have a better idea of what characterizes love, we need to be aware of some specific ways in which love expresses itself. In these verses Paul provides us with eight examples of love at work. Each illustration is in the form of a directive. We are exhorted to put our beliefs about Christian love into practice—especially in our relationships with other believers. So as we probe further into Paul's words, let's contemplate how we can better achieve God's standard of love.

1. **Devotion** (v. 10a). This passage calls on us to "be devoted to one another in brotherly love." The Greek word rendered *devoted* means "full of tenderness." It conveys the idea of the deep affection felt and abiding commitment made between natural family members, such as parents and children. The Greek term *philadelphía* literally means "brother love." Paul's use of these two terms shows us that the love Christians are to express in their spiritual family should exhibit the same loving qualities that are often shared in their physical family.
2. **Unselfishness** (v. 10b). We are also told to "give preference to one another in honor." When we love as we should, we will esteem others more highly than ourselves and readily give them the honor they deserve (cf. Phil. 2:3–4, 1 Thess. 5:12–13).
3. **Enthusiasm** (v. 11). Sincere love involves "not lagging behind in diligence" but possessing a fervency in spirit as the Lord is served. We are not to be lazy or indifferent in our Christian service. Instead, we should engage in the work of love with enthusiasm and delight.
4. **Hopefulness** (v. 12a). Our love should manifest itself as we rejoice "in hope." As believers, our horizons should never be bound by the visible and the temporal or the past and the present. Our hope lies in the glory of God (Rom. 5:2) that we will one day experience when we are fully renewed into the image of Christ (John 1:14, Col. 3:10–11, 1 John 3:2). Indeed, so great will be our

enjoyment of God's glory that the event is referred to as our glorification (Rom. 8:17, 21, 29–30). No wonder we can rejoice! God is in the process of remaking us, and He will not stop until we are as much like His Son as we possibly can be (cf. Phil. 1:6).

5. **Consistency** (v. 12b). Real love also displays the ability to persevere in the midst of adversity and trial. When people are difficult to get along with—even resistant to truth—Christian love has resilience and staying power that keeps building bridges and breaking down walls.
6. **Prayerfulness** (v. 12c). Believers who genuinely love are "devoted to prayer." While on their knees before God, they will consistently bring the needs of their family, friends, associates, and enemies to Him in intercessory and petitionary prayer. A beautiful example of one Christian who exemplified this love-act is Stephen. When he was being stoned by the crowd he had preached to, he cried out to God, asking Him not to hold his executioners' sin against them (Acts 7:60). A man who at that time approved of Stephen's stoning and heard his prayer was Saul. He later became one of the greatest apostles of the church. We know him today as Paul, the human author of many letters in the New Testament.
7. **Generosity** (v. 13a). Those who love authentically express their care by "contributing to the needs of the saints." Christians are responsible to help meet any needs fellow believers might have. This includes giving assistance in spiritual, psychological, physical, and financial matters. When we fail to help in such areas, we display our lack of love. The Apostle John made this point very clear when he wrote: "But whoever has the world's goods, and beholds his brother in need and closes his heart against him, how does the love of God abide in him? Little children, let us not love with word or with tongue, but in deed and truth" (1 John 3:17–18).
8. **Hospitality** (v. 13b). As Christians, we are called to express our love to others by "practicing hospitality." The Greek term for *hospitality* means "affection to strangers." Simply because we may not know certain people or name them among our friends does not give us a license to ignore or slight them. On the contrary, we should openly invite them into our lives and express to them the sincere kindness of divine love.

III. Why Love Stops.

It would certainly be wonderful if the love of which Paul has spoken was exhibited more abundantly and consistently among us. The Lord has given us all the resources we need for such an outpouring, but it still doesn't happen. Why not? The fault lies with us. We keep love from flowing as it should. But why don't we love as we ought? Among the many reasons we could name, three are predominant. Once we recognize and deal with them, we will begin to see love freely overflowing in our personal and corporate lives.

A. **Because We Are Afraid.** We are fearful of being rejected, misunderstood, or ignored, so we keep a safe distance between ourselves and others. This displays a lack of security that can be overcome by realizing our everlasting acceptance and inestimable value in Christ.

B. **Because We Are Passive.** We like to be told what to do. We naturally look for an acknowledged expert, a set of directions, or an established formula to guide us through our endeavors. This squelches spontaneity and ignores the nature of love. Love is creative and active. Thus, in order to love others, we need to feel free to vigorously reach out in novel as well as proven ways.

C. **Because We Are Preoccupied.** We don't like to be bothered or interrupted. But some of love's greatest opportunities come at the most inconvenient times. Rather than being insensitive during those occasions, we should be alert to their occurrences and stand ready as God's ministers of love.

Living Insights

Study One

In Romans 12:9, we learned that real love is *unhypocritical* and *discriminating.* From the verses that followed, we gleaned some insight into the accompanying objectives of Christian love. Let's focus on these latter qualities in this study.

- After copying the chart below, use a Bible concordance to start looking up the words listed in the left column. Once you jot down where each word occurs in Scripture, go back and read the references. Then, in the other column, write a one-sentence summary of what each reference may tell you about the love-quality listed.

Accompanying Objectives of Love		
Words	Passages	Summary Statements
Devoted		On Devotion
Preference		On Unselfishness
Fervent		On Enthusiasm
Hope		On Hopefulness
Persevering		On Consistency
Prayer		On Prayerfulness
Contributing		On Generosity
Hospitality		On Hospitality

Living Insights

Study Two

This lesson concluded with three reasons love ceases to express itself in our lives. Take a few minutes to personally consider each of these by honestly answering the following questions.

- How do fear and insecurity demonstrate themselves in my life?
- In what areas of my life am I so inactive and uncreative that I squelch the effectiveness of love?
- What things tend to preoccupy me so that I fail to demonstrate love to others?
- How can I turn these hindrances around so that something positive results?

You and Your Enemy

Romans 12:14–21

The Apostle Paul consistently addresses areas in our lives that need attention. At times, however, his pen cuts like a scalpel as it performs spiritual and relational surgery on us. The closing verses of Romans 12 stand as a valid case in point. In this section of Scripture we are confronted with our relationship to our enemies. The reaction of our flesh is to be ready to strike back at our foes whenever they threaten us in any way. And when we return blows, we often take delight in getting even. Through the words of Paul, God counteracts this natural reaction with a supernatural response of love. If we will listen to His voice and heed His counsel even in regard to our enemies, then we will gain the opportunity to experience love's rewards.

I. Some Basic Facts to Remember.

As we examine these verses and allow them to start operating in our lives, we need to keep two essential thoughts in mind. First, *this passage is personal, not national.* Paul is not dealing with relationships between countries or communities. Instead, he is giving instruction on how individual believers should relate to those persons who, for some reason, have become their enemies. Second, *the counsel in this passage is attainable, not idealistic.* Romans 12:14–21 is sandwiched between achievable teaching on how we should dedicate ourselves to God (12:1–3), manifest unity through the harmonious use of diverse gifts (12:4–8), exercise love toward one another (12:9–13), and yield to governmental authorities (13:1–7). Of course, we cannot obey this instruction by our own natural powers. However, all of the imperatives directed toward believers can be kept through the empowering ministry of the Holy Spirit. He can and will help us do what we are unable to accomplish on our own.

II. Some Needed Insight from Romans 12.

We are now ready to be wheeled into the operating room to gain from first-hand experience the surgical insights of verses 14–21. Prepare yourself! The truths we are about to discover will penetrate our spirits; but what they are seeking to remove from our lives will make us healthier Christians.

A. Initial Insight: Counteract your natural, human instincts (v. 14). Some of our innate tendencies are good. For example, when we begin to fall forward, we instinctively stretch out our hands so as to cushion the fall and protect us from harm. However, we have other natural reactions that are detrimental. When we verbally lash out at a person who has delivered to us a sarcastic jab, we are acting wrongfully. The Lord does not want us to follow our natural instincts in such situations. Rather, He exhorts us to obey a supernatural injunction—namely, "Bless those who persecute you; bless and curse not." We are told to speak well of those who criticize and slander us. Indeed, whether we like it or not, our enemies' hurtful words often convey insightful truths about our characters. As painful as it may be, we can grow through the attacks of our critics. But whether or not we find benefit in what they say, we are called on by God to be gracious to them.

B. **Personal Insight: Put yourself in your enemy's place** (vv. 15–16). This truth is embedded in these exhortations: "Rejoice with those who rejoice, and weep with those who weep. Be of the same mind toward one another; do not be haughty in mind, but associate with the lowly. Do not be wise in your own estimation." When someone assaults our faith, ability, character, integrity, or any other thing we seek to protect, God desires that we view the charges from their perspective. We are not exhorted to defend ourselves simply because we are under personal attack. Such an action would only alienate us from our enemies. Rather, we are instructed to view life from the vantage point of our persecutors. This response will give us the equilibrium and insight we need to communicate in a loving, unselfish way.

C. **Relational Insight: Look for your enemy's good and support it** (vv. 17–18). When we think of our enemies, we tend to focus on their weaknesses. Then, as attacks come and our enemies' poorer qualities are exposed, we often take advantage of the opportunity to strike back with "constructive" assaults on their character. God is opposed to this tactic. He commands us to "never pay back evil for evil to anyone." Instead, He desires that we "respect what is right in the sight of all men." Rather than fix our attention on the evil habits, traits, tactics, and jabs of our enemies, we are to search for the good in their lives and encourage its presence and development. This approach will make it much easier to carry out the command in verse 18, "If possible, so far as it depends on you, be at peace with all men." God tells us to do everything we can to promote harmony in our relationships with others, be they friends or foes. However, He is wise enough to know that even the best of efforts will not always bring about a favorable response. But our task is not to force change on others. We are exhorted to allow God to change us so that peace might have an opportunity to prevail in all our relationships.

D. **Vertical Insight: Leave all revenge to God** (v. 19). The text makes this point quite clear: "Never take your own revenge, beloved, but leave room for the wrath of God, for it is written,

'Vengeance is Mine, I will repay,' says the Lord." When attacked, our natural reaction is to retaliate. But the Lord's desire is that we refuse to yield to this temptation by placing our trust in His promise to defend us. Of course, His timing and method may drastically differ from ours. However, we may rest assured that He will not allow us to suffer unduly. An Old Testament illustration of this principle occurs in 2 Samuel 16. Read the account slowly and reflectively.

> When King David came to Bahurim, behold, there came out from there a man of the family of the house of Saul whose name was Shimei, the son of Gera; he came out cursing continually as he came. And he threw stones at David and at all the servants of King David; and all the people and all the mighty men were at his right hand and at his left. And thus Shimei said when he cursed, "Get out, get out, you man of bloodshed, and worthless fellow! The Lord has returned upon you all the bloodshed of the house of Saul, in whose place you have reigned; and the Lord has given the kingdom into the hand of your son Absalom. And behold, you are taken in your own evil, for you are a man of bloodshed!" Then Abishai the son of Zeruiah said to the king, "Why should this dead dog curse my lord the king? Let me go over now, and cut off his head." But the king said, "What have I to do with you, O sons of Zeruiah? If he curses, and if the Lord has told him, 'Curse David,' then who shall say, 'Why have you done so?'" Then David said to Abishai and to all his servants, "Behold, my son who came out from me seeks my life; how much more now this Benjamite? Let him alone and let him curse, for the Lord has told him. Perhaps the Lord will look on my affliction and return good to me instead of his cursing this day." So David and his men went on the way; and Shimei went along on the hillside parallel with him and as he went he cursed, and cast stones and threw dust at him. (2 Sam. 16:5–13)

We do not need to defend ourselves. If we are in the right, then God will exonerate us. And if we are in the wrong, then we may expect the Lord to convict us. But we should be prepared, for He may even use our enemies to expose our errors.

E. Practical Insight: Be sensitive to your enemy's needs and meet them (v. 20). This is an imperative many of us balk at, but it is thoroughly grounded in Scripture. Consider these words: " 'But if your enemy is hungry, feed him, and if he is thirsty, give him a drink; for in so doing you will heap burning coals upon his head.' " The latter part of this text does not mean that we should strive to help our enemies with a motive of revenge. That notion was rebuked in the previous verse. Rather, the passage is teaching that when we respond to personal assaults with genuine love, our acts of kindness will bring a burning sense of shame and guilt to our enemies.

III. A Foundational Formula of Love.

The closing verse of Romans 12 affirms the fact that *love is always victorious.* The passage teaches this by giving us two final exhortations in regard to dealing with our enemies.

A. Do not become a victim of evil (v. 21a). When we allow ourselves to be overcome by the assaults of those who oppose us, we become a casualty of the very evil we struggle against.

B. Conquer evil with good (v. 21b). In personal relationships, love is the one weapon we have that God has sanctified for our use. Indeed, when we pull it from its sheath and wield it as the Lord has commanded, He will grant us victory and perhaps even turn our enemies into friends. But one thing is certain—love is the only response that finds favor with God. The Apostle Peter expresses this truth well:

> For this finds favor, if for the sake of conscience toward God a man bears up under sorrows when suffering unjustly. For what credit is there if, when you sin and are harshly treated, you endure it with patience? But if when you do what is right and suffer for it you patiently endure it, this finds favor with God. For you have been called for this purpose, since Christ also suffered for you, leaving you an example for you to follow in His steps, who committed no sin, nor was any deceit found in His mouth; and while being reviled, He did not revile in return; while suffering, He uttered no threats, but kept entrusting Himself to Him who judges righteously. (1 Pet. 2:19–23)

Living Insights

Study One

This entire chapter is a marvelous tapestry with many individual threads wonderfully woven together. Let's try our hand at weaving our own version of Romans 12.

- Reread Romans 12:1–21. Take a piece of paper from your notebook and write out this chapter *in your own words.* Zero in on the thoughts and feelings embedded in the printed text. And don't forget to make your paraphrase personal by plugging your name into the appropriate spots.

Living Insights

Study Two

Did you notice the title of this lesson? It's "You and Your Enemy." Let's get uncomfortably personal: Who is *your* enemy? How can you apply the healing balm of Romans 12 to your relationship with your enemy? Use a copy of the following chart to help you map out a biblical strategy.

Strategy for Loving My Enemy		
My Enemy's Frame of Reference	My Enemy's Good Points	My Enemy's Needs

How to Be a Godly Rebel

Romans 13:1–7

Throughout history God's people have often found themselves in an ethical dilemma. The Bible commands us to obey the Lord. The Scriptures also instruct us to submit to human governing authorities. But what should we do when the two commands come into conflict? Should we yield to the biblical injunctions to obey God, or should we follow the equally authoritative imperatives to obey the civil government? Does the Bible give us any help in resolving this issue? It certainly does! And although we will be unable to examine all of the biblical texts that concern this matter, we will have an opportunity to delve into some of the most crucial ones. Among these passages, Romans 13:1–7 is probably the most important as well as the least understood. So let's lay our opinions and prejudices aside and hear afresh God's counsel on this timely topic.

I. Four Difficult Dilemmas.

An excellent way to gain an appreciation for the troublesome questions raised by this issue is to place ourselves in some situations that highlight the problem. There are four periods in history that will serve this function well. Let's imaginatively transport ourselves back in time and slip into the shoes of some Christians who faced the very real dilemma of obeying either God or their government.

A. The American Revolutionary War. Picture yourself as a believer in the young colonies of eighteenth-century America. You are living under the political authority of England. There is a good deal of talk about breaking away from this government, even if it results in military action. Soon you find yourself in the midst of a revolution. Should you support it in any way? Is there clear, biblical warrant for the revolt? Or does Scripture enjoin you to remain obedient to the dictates of England?

B. The American Civil War. Now step back into the time tunnel and move forward to the late 1850s and early 1860s. You're the owner of a large plantation in the Deep South. As a Christian, you struggle with the issue of slavery. However, in order to keep yourself in business, you have continued to use slave labor as the chief means for maintaining crop production. Eventually, you read in the newspaper that the South has taken military action to secede from the Union. One of the key issues involves the whole question of slavery. And although, theologically, you find yourself aligned with those who want to abolish slavery, politically, you are now under a government that has chosen to defend the slave owners—among whom you are one! What should you do? Should you align yourself with the North or the South? And on what biblical grounds are you going to base your decision?

C. Nazi Germany. You are now a Christian politician in Germany during the 1930s. A new leader has come into power. His name is Adolf Hitler. He has contacted you to ask if you would accept a high-ranking position in his Third Reich. But you recall Hitler's attitude and prejudiced treatment toward the Jews in your land. As a Christian, you find that his view of the Jews contradicts the biblical teaching about the intrinsic worth of every human being. However, you also remember numerous instances in Scripture where believers maintained authoritative positions in governments that did not perpetuate Christian values. Indeed, these believers were able to help alleviate suffering and injustice because they remained active in their civil jobs (for examples, see Gen. 41:38–50:21 and the books of Nehemiah and Daniel). Thus, should you accept or reject Hitler's offer? And if you accept, are you then committed to yielding to his policies concerning the Jews? In fact, as a citizen of Germany, are you not under both political and biblical obligation to obey your government's laws regardless of what they are?

D. Today's Russia. The time tunnel has just transported you forward to our present time period. However, you are not in a country where religious freedom is allowed. Indeed, this country's government has made it illegal for a citizen to possess a Bible. You have arrived in the Soviet Union. Here you are a trusted official in an industrial plant. As such, you are expected to support the policies of the Communist party. However, you have just received an underground message that a group of Christians outside of Russia's borders need you to help them smuggle Bibles into the country. Should you break the law and give these Christians the aid they need? Or should you obey the law and expose their operation to the governmental authorities?

II. Two Familiar Extremes.

When Christians are faced with dilemmas such as these, they often respond in one of two unbalanced ways. The first extreme could be referred to as *inappropriate independence.* Christians who take this approach display an antigovernment militance that virtually disregards established authority. They are quick to protest, violate civil laws, and even take up arms to defend their independence. The second imbalanced response may be called *uninvolved indifference.* Christians who adopt this position practically never step into the governmental arena. They insist that civil involvement is tantamount to polishing the rails on a sinking ship . . . it will do no everlasting good. "Besides," they say, "since Christ will come soon for believers, there is no reason to try to alter current laws so that they will align better with Christian standards. For when He raptures believers from the face of the earth, the Great Tribulation will begin and the Antichrist will reign. This event will destroy any good we might now accomplish in the political sphere." Although these two responses are common among Christians today, we shall see that both are clear violations of biblical teaching.

III. One Primary Principle.

As we prepare to examine the teaching found in Romans 13:1–7, we need to be aware of a central truth grounded in Scripture. The principle is this: *A Christian's disobedience of civil authority is justified when that authority requires him or her to disobey God.* Two sections in the Bible that exemplify this principle occur back-to-back in Acts. And though they record different events, the issue they raise is the same: Are believers morally obligated to obey God or human institutions when the laws of both come into conflict? The resounding answer is that believers must obey God in such situations rather than man. In Acts 4, the Jewish religious leaders commanded Peter and John "not to speak or teach at all in the name of Jesus" (v. 18). But the two apostles refused to submit to their authority on this matter (vv. 19–20). As a consequence, the Holy Spirit gave them the power "to speak the word of God" with even greater boldness than they had before (v. 31). In Acts 5, the Jewish religious authorities again confronted Peter and the other apostles concerning their disobedience of human authority. To this "Peter and the apostles answered and said, 'We must obey God rather than men'" (v. 29). In instances like these, a Christian is obligated to be a godly rebel.

IV. Some Biblical Guidelines.

With all of this information in mind, we are now ready to probe into Romans 13:1–7. As we peruse the passage, it becomes readily apparent that the central thought conveyed is this: *A good Christian is a good citizen.* God expects His people to "be in subjection to the governing authorities" (v. 1a). Why? Because "there is no authority except from God, and those which exist are established by God" (v. 1b). This does not mean that everything a given government does is right. Nor does this instruction imply that it is always wrong to disobey the dictates of one's government. What this verse does reveal is that individuals within a country are not sanctioned by God to establish themselves as civil authorities. Instead, He has chosen to place individuals under governments that He has raised up for His own purposes (cf. Jer. 27:5–8; Dan. 2:21, 4:31–32). Among the many issues this raises, two are directly addressed in verses 2–7 of Romans 13.

A. The Issue of Inappropriate Resistance (vv. 2–5). In these verses we are given three reasons for not resisting the proper exercise of governmental authority. The first one is theological:

God supports law and order. As the beginning of verse 2 states, "Therefore he who resists authority has opposed the ordinance of God." When we break an established law that does not violate the clear teaching of Scripture, then we are in effect disobeying the Ruler over all. The second reason given is an external one: *Civil disobedience brings severe consequences.* The text informs us that "they who have opposed [governmental authorities] will receive condemnation upon themselves" (v. 2b). This will occur because "rulers are not a cause of fear for good behavior, but for evil" (v. 3a). So if we do not want to be afraid of suffering penalties exacted by the state for civil disobedience, then we had better obey the established laws (vv. 3b–4). The third reason we should not inappropriately resist state dictates is an internal one: *Our consciences will become intolerable.* We will struggle through inner turmoil if we wrongfully disobey the laws of the land (Rom. 13:5; cf. 2 Sam. 11–12, Ps. 32:1–5). But we help maintain a guilt-free conscience when we keep the established laws.

B. The Issue of Appropriate Obedience (vv. 6–7). These verses in Romans 13 utilize the subject of taxes as an illustration of how we should submit to governmental leaders and laws. Very simply, we are told to pay our taxes (v. 6). The first part of the seventh verse expands upon this command: "Render to all what is due them: tax [i.e., for personal property] to whom tax is due; custom [i.e., for importing and exporting goods] to whom custom." Whatever the government can rightfully claim, it should receive. As Jesus Christ says, " 'Render to Caesar the things that are Caesar's, and to God the things that are God's' " (Mark 12:17a). Furthermore, the Lord exhorts us to render "fear [i.e., respect] to whom fear" is due and "honor [i.e., allegiance] to whom honor" is due (Rom. 13:7b). Granted, God is the One who should receive our ultimate expression of respect and allegiance. However, that same King also commands us to show a lesser though important commitment to our civil authorities. Therefore, when we obey the established human officials, we are also obeying God.

V. A Personal Response.

From what we have studied, we can see that our Christian response to God and civil government is twofold.

A. We are to obey God always. He is our ultimate Source of authority and therefore the One to whom we owe our ultimate allegiance.

B. We are to obey the government usually. Only when the governing authorities overstep their divinely established boundaries do we have any basis for civil disobedience. And when such a situation arises, we are still bound by God to obey all the governmental directives that do not run contrary to His Word.

Living Insights

Study One

When should Christians obey their government? When should they disobey? We need to grasp several passages of Scripture in order to give accurate answers.

- The following chart contains many of the major passages in which the civil obedience/disobedience issue is addressed. After you carefully read each reference, summarize your thoughts in the right column.

Civil Obedience/Disobedience	
Scripture References	Summary Statements
Exodus 1:8–21	
Exodus 2:11–15	
Daniel 3	
Daniel 6	
Mark 12:13–17	
Acts 4:1–31	
Acts 5:12–42	
Acts 16:35–40	
Romans 13:1–7	
Titus 3:1	
1 Peter 2:13–17	

Living Insights

Study Two

The Apostle Paul writes these wise words in his first letter to Timothy: "First of all, then, I urge that entreaties and prayers, petitions and thanksgivings, be made on behalf of all men, for kings and all who are in authority, in order that we may lead a tranquil and quiet life in all godliness and dignity" (1 Tim. 2:1–2).

- Let's spend some time in prayer for our government. Turn to God and intercede on behalf of your community and national leaders. Be as specific as possible in your requests, asking Him to work out His perfect will in their personal lives and political responsibilities.

Digging Deeper

The subject of the Christian's relationship with civil government always raises difficult but important questions. Here is just a small sampling: Should believers ever disobey their governing authorities? If so, then under what conditions and by what means are they obligated to do so? Should Christians ever resort to violence as a method for expressing their disobedience toward human authority or bringing about desired changes in government? Is there any biblical warrant for Christians to engage in or support a revolution within their country or the countries of others? Do Christians have any responsibilities to their governments and communities? If so, what are they and how should they be carried out? Should Christians try to alter government policies and laws so that they conform to biblical standards? Or should believers work to preserve the rights of others to live contrary to scriptural principles if they so choose? If you would like to dig deeper into these questions in order to unearth some biblical answers, then we would encourage you to consult the many resource tools listed below. These references will supply you with the numerous scriptural passages and principles that are relevant to this issue. They will also introduce you to the different positions Christians have taken on these passages, as well as on the issues of Christian social responsibility and civil disobedience. The thinkers represented here will sometimes disagree, but your job is to evaluate what they say in light of the biblical record. So don't take their interpretations of the scriptural texts for granted. Instead, conduct your own study of the passages in question. This will help you in assessing the validity of their views.

- **Resource Tools on Social Responsibility and Civil Disobedience.**

Andrew, Brother. *Is Life So Dear?* Nashville: Thomas Nelson Publishers, 1985.

Bloesch, Donald G. *Crumbling Foundations: Death and Rebirth in an Age of Upheaval.* Academie Books. Grand Rapids: Zondervan Publishing House, 1984.

Buzzard, Lynn. *With Liberty and Justice.* Wheaton: Victor Books, 1984.

Buzzard, Lynn, and Campbell, Paula. *Holy Disobedience: When Christians Must Resist the State.* Ann Arbor: Servant Books, 1984.

Campolo, Anthony. *Ideas for Social Action.* Edited by Wayne Rice. Youth Specialties. Grand Rapids: Zondervan Publishing House, 1983.

Conlan, John and Irene. *Beyond 1984.* Scottsdale: FaithAmerica Press, Inc., n. d.

Eidsmoe, John. *God and Caesar: Christian Faith and Political* Action. Westchester: Crossway Books, 1984.

Frizen, Edwin L., Jr., and Coggins, Wade T., editors. *Christ and Caesar in Christian Missions.* Pasadena: William Carey Library, 1979.

Geisler, Norman L. "A Biblical View of Government." *The Rutherford Institute* 2:1 (January/February 1985), pp. 8–9, 12.

Geisler, Norman L. "A Premillennial View of Law and Government." *Bibliotheca Sacra* 142:567 (July–September 1985), pp. 250–66.

Geisler, Norman L. *Ethics: Alternatives and Issues.* Foreword by Harold B. Kuhn. Grand Rapids: Zondervan Publishing House, 1971. See especially chaps. 7, 9, 10, 13, 14.

Goldberg, George. *Reconsecrating America.* Grand Rapids: William B. Eerdmans Publishing Co., 1984.

Henry, Carl F. H. *The Christian Mindset in a Secular Society: Promoting Evangelical Renewal and National Righteousness.* Portland: Multnomah Press, 1984.

Hinchliff, Peter. *Holiness and Politics.* Grand Rapids: William B. Eerdmans Publishing Co., 1982.

Longenecker, Richard N. *New Testament Social Ethics for Today.* Grand Rapids: William B. Eerdmans Publishing Co., 1984.

Monsma, Stephen V. *Pursuing Justice in a Sinful World.* Grand Rapids: William B. Eerdmans Publishing Co., 1984.

Montgomery, John Warwick. "The Limits of Christian Influence." *Christianity Today* 25:2 (January 23, 1981), pp. 60, 63.

Niebuhr, H. Richard. *Christ and Culture.* New York: Harper & Brothers Publishers, 1951. Niebuhr was not a theologically conservative Christian. However, this particular book by him has been so influential on conservative Christian thinkers that we would be amiss if we excluded it.

Noll, Mark A.; Hatch, Nathan O.; and Marsden, George M. *The Search for Christian America.* Westchester: Crossway Books, 1983.

Ryrie, Charles C. *What You Should Know about Social*

Responsibility. Current Christian Issues. Chicago: Moody Press, 1982.

Schlossberg, Herbert. *Idols for Destruction: Christian Faith and Its Confrontation with American Society.* Nashville: Thomas Nelson Publishers, 1983.

Stott, John. *Involvement: Being a Responsible Christian in a Non-Christian Society.* A Crucial Questions Book. Old Tappan: Fleming H. Revell Co., 1984.

Stott, John R. W., editor. *The Year 2000.* Downers Grove: InterVarsity Press, 1983.

Vos, Johannes G. "The Social and Economic Responsibility of the Visible Church." *Westminster Theological Journal* 10 (1948), pp. 107–38.

Webber, Robert E. *The Secular Saint: The Role of the Christian in the Secular World.* Academie Books. Grand Rapids: Zondervan Publishing House, 1979.

Whitehead, John W. *The Right to Picket and the Freedom of Public Discourse.* The Rutherford Institute Report: Vol. 3. Westchester: Crossway Books, 1984.

Whitehead, John W. *The Separation Illusion: A Lawyer Examines the First Amendment.* Foreword by R. J. Rushdoony. Milford: Mott Media, 1977.

Whitehead, John W. *The Stealing of America.* Westchester: Crossway Books, 1983.

Wolterstorff, Nicholas. *Until Justice and Peace Embrace.* Grand Rapids: William B. Eerdmans Publishing Co., 1983.

Legal Tender and Loving Care

Romans 13:8–10

From Romans 12 on, Paul begins to more fully apply the theology that he has so carefully spelled out in the previous chapters. In this final section of the letter, we are given wise counsel regarding our personal relationships with others. Paul informs us about how to serve others (12:3–8), love without hypocrisy (12:9–13), treat our enemies (12:14–21), and relate to government (13:1–4). In the middle verses of chapter 13, Paul gives us equally valuable instruction on how to handle our debts and love other people. During the present era of financial strain and relational selfishness, we need to hear and heed these wise words from Romans.

I. The Context.

We always run the risk of misinterpreting a biblical passage when we fail to consider the verses that surround it. So let's briefly remind ourselves of the context of Romans 13. Generally speaking, this chapter is found in a section that deals with how to live the Christian life. Specifically, verses 8–10 of this chapter flow from an immediate context concerning a Christian's responsibility to be a good citizen (vv. 1–7). Here the central instruction is that an upstanding citizen is one who submits to the governing authorities as long as they don't contradict God's Word.

II. The Issues.

Now that we have the context in mind, let's get an overview of the issues covered in Romans 13:8–10. The first subject is *paying what is due.* It concerns financial debts not to governments but to individuals, businesses, and agencies. The second issue is *demonstrating what is best.* This has to do with our debt of love. The final matter addressed is *fulfilling what is commanded.* Here the focus is on the law.

III. The Meaning.

We can get a handle on these three issues by analyzing the individual phrases in verses 8–10. As we do this, let's remain vulnerable to what God desires to teach us.

A. "Owe nothing to anyone" (v. 8a). In this verse the Greek verb for *owe* is in the present tense. Consequently, the command literally reads, "Do not keep owing anyone anything." In other words, when a payment is due on a bill, we are told to pay it. If we fail to meet our financial obligations, then we violate this biblical injunction. Please notice that a proper use of credit is not prohibited here. Rather, we are exhorted to consistently and appropriately meet our economic debts. When we do, the name of Christ will be honored instead of defamed.

B. "Love one another" (v. 8b). The only debt we have that can never be fully paid is love for one another. Of course, it is usually easy to love those who are in the family of God. After all, Christians have the same Father, embrace the same Savior, submit to the same Spirit, and seek to obey the same Bible. But what about non-Christians? Are we to love them also? Yes! Notice what Paul wrote, "For he who loves his neighbor has fulfilled the law." When Paul commanded us to love one another, he used the term *ǎllos,* which means "another of the same kind." However, in his exhortation to love our neighbors, he used the Greek word *héteros,* which means "another of a different kind." In short, we are to demonstrate an unselfish love toward those who have different beliefs, tastes, values, and mannerisms than we do. God wants believers to reach out to everyone, regardless of any differences that may exist. A wonderful example of this truth is found in James 2. While reading through these pertinent verses, reflect on how you treat people in your home, church, and place of business.

> My brethren, do not hold your faith in our glorious Lord Jesus Christ with an attitude of personal favoritism. For if a man comes into your assembly with a gold ring and dressed in fine clothes, and there also comes in a poor man in dirty clothes, and you pay special attention to the one who is wearing the fine clothes, and say, "You sit here in a good place," and you say to the poor man, "You stand over there, or sit down by my footstool," have you not made distinctions among yourselves, and become judges with evil motives? Listen, my beloved brethren: did not God choose the poor of this world to be rich in faith and heirs of the kingdom which He promised to those who love Him? But you have dishonored the poor man. . . . If, however, you are fulfilling the royal law, according to the Scripture, "You shall love your neighbor as yourself," you are doing well. But if you show partiality, you are committing sin and are convicted by the law as transgressors. (James 2:1–6a, 8–9)

C. "He . . . has fulfilled the law" (vv. 8c–9a). In these verses from Romans Paul adds that the Christian who loves others indiscriminately has "fulfilled the law." This does not mean that the Apostle is placing believers back under the demands of the Old Testament Law. Rather, he is saying that this kind of love is the same type that undergirds and permeates the Law (Gal. 5:14) as well as all other portions of Scripture. Therefore, when we love others as God loves them, we are fulfilling the very essence of the Lord's commands to us. Furthermore, Christian love will exemplify itself in a number of specific ways. Paul lists some of them for us: "For this [or better yet, because of this], 'You shall not commit adultery, you shall not murder, you shall not steal, you shall not covet' " (Rom. 13:9a). Paul is not giving a series of commands here, but he is stating in a negative way that authentic love seeks what is best. If we really love someone, we will not take advantage of that person's mate, life, or belongings. Instead, we will do whatever we can to benefit his or her life to the greatest degree. That's real love in action!

D. "Love your neighbor as yourself" (vv. 9b–10). We reach the zenith of our love for others when we love them as fully as we should love ourselves. A healthy, wholesome individual will not try to harm himself; rather, he will seek to take care of himself. But he will not do so at the expense of another's well being (cf. Eph. 5:28–29). A person who loves himself in this manner is free to do good for other people. However, individuals who dislike themselves will usually transfer that hatred to others. It should go without saying that this self-love is to be marked not by an inflated ego but by the realization that we are being renewed into Christ's holy image. This fact presupposes that we are still sinners in daily need of God's grace and mercy.

IV. The Relevance.

There are three abiding principles that emerge from the counsel in these verses.

A. Only one continuing debt can honor the Lord: loving the other person.

B. Only one penetrating command can fulfill the law: loving the person that is different.

C. Only one liberating truth can release Christian love: loving ourselves in a biblical manner.

Living Insights

Study One

For some of us, the toughest area of life to give God is our *finances*. Before we yield to the temptation of passing by this topic, let's consider some more financial principles from God's Word.

- The following chart lists several verses in Proverbs that address the area of finances. After you copy it into your notebook, write a principle that is suggested in each reference.

You and Your Finances	
Scripture References	Financial Principles
Proverbs	
10:15	
10:22	
11:4	
13:7	
14:20	
14:31	
19:17	
22:2	
23:5	
28:20	

Living Insights

Study Two

How does your current financial picture measure up to God's standards? Copy the following charts into your notebook and jot down some observations of your situation. Be sure to include current strengths, weaknesses, and areas which need further improvement.

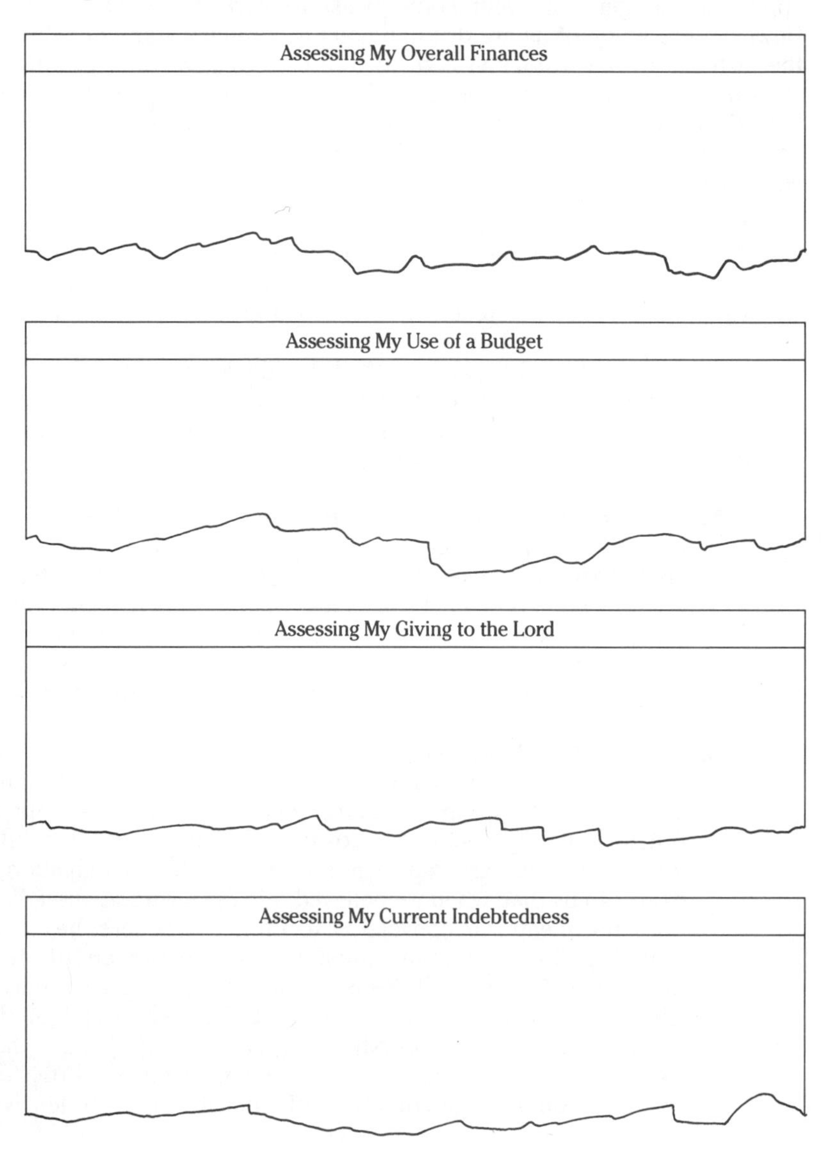

Wake Up and Get Dressed!

Romans 13:11–14

Some of us have little difficulty waking up in the morning after a good night's rest. Others of us struggle getting our eyes to focus and our minds to function in the first hours of the morning. What is true physically also applies in the spiritual realm. Some of us are alert and active spiritually. However, too many of us are drifting along in a religious stupor, allowing the fashions of the world's system to ruin our lives. We who are in this state need to wake up, shed our ungodly clothing, and put on Christ. That is Paul's message in Romans 13:11–14. Let's pay special regard to what he has to say, for it has a crucial bearing on how we should live in a world gone awry.

I. Our Alarm Sounds.

Paul conveys his instruction through the sights and sounds of an early morning awakening. The bit of imagery he draws on in verse 11 is what we would refer to as an alarm. However, he is referring not to a physical alarm but to a spiritual one sounded by God. Paul expresses the thought this way: "And this do, knowing the time, that it is already the hour for you to awaken from sleep; for now salvation is nearer to us than when we believed" (v. 11). There are two aspects of this verse that open up its message. Let's examine them as they occur in the passage.

A. Checking the Time (v. 11a). Paul tells us that the hour is late. Because of this, we are to exercise Christian love to believers and unbelievers alike (vv. 8–10). The *time* to which he refers is not the hour marked by a clock but the epoch or period of history in which one lives. We Christians are exhorted to understand our times and observe that our generation is asleep in spiritual darkness. The non-Christians who surround us need to be awakened by the light of love that we can shine.

B. Awakening from Sleep (v. 11b). But we cannot shake our generation from slumber until we "awaken from sleep." We must arise from our spiritual lethargy before we can reach out to others. But why should we do it now? Can't we sleep a little longer? No, answers Paul. The reason is that "now salvation is nearer to us than when we believed." By the term *salvation,* Paul does not mean our conversion to Christ. Therefore, he is not teaching that Christians must remain unsure about their born-again status until Jesus Christ comes to take them to Himself. Instead, Paul is saying that the last aspect of the salvation process is closer to being consummated than when we first trusted in Christ as our Savior. In other words, the resurrection and glorification of our physical bodies will occur at the return of Jesus Christ (Rom. 8:22–23, Heb. 9:28, 1 Pet. 1:3–9). And because His coming is imminent, we need to be alert and vigilant spiritually (Mark 13:28–37, James 5:8).

II. Our Day Begins.

As our eyes open and our minds begin to function, we become more aware that the evening is almost over and the morning is about to dawn. At that juncture, we begin to face reality and start dressing appropriately for the day. This familiar picture is what Paul uses to continue his exhortation. Let's closely consider its key elements.

A. Accepting Reality (v. 12a). Here we read that "the night is almost gone, and the day is at hand." What Paul means by *night* and *day* is illuminated by the words of Jesus in John 9. In that chapter we are told about a man Jesus saw who had been "blind from birth" (John 9:1). Christ's disciples asked Him, " 'Who sinned, this man or his parents, that he should be born blind?' " Jesus responded by explaining that neither personal nor parental sin was the cause. Rather, he was born blind " 'in order that the works of God might be displayed in him' " (vv. 2–3). From this point, Jesus went on to say, " 'We must work the works of Him who sent Me, as long as it is day; night is coming, when no man can work. While I am in the world, I am the light of the world' " (vv. 4–5). Put another way, while Jesus was on earth, He manifested the light of the tangible presence of God. But when He ascended to heaven, the light He had displayed grew dim on our planet. The physical manifestation of God was gone, and with it, the divine Source of light. However, not all light has been removed; reflected light still remains. Just as the moon reflects the physical light of the sun, so Christians reflect the spiritual light of the Savior. Consequently, while we are still on the earth, we need to illumine the world with the light we have. For soon the Lord Jesus Christ will return for us. And when He does, a new day of glory will dawn for believers, but a dark night of judgment will come upon unbelievers. We need to face these facts and diligently be about our Father's business.

B. Changing Clothes (v. 12b). Once we awake to the reality that Christ's return is imminent, we need to "lay aside the deeds of darkness and put on the armor of light" (Rom. 13:12b). It is inappropriate and immoral for children of light to clothe themselves with a lifestyle that befits the world of darkness. God's people should wear the protective garments of a holy lifestyle, not the fashionable yet destructive clothing of a sinful manner of life.

III. Our Lives Displayed.

In verses 13–14, Paul goes on to clarify how we should and should not live as we actively await Christ's return.

A. Inappropriate Behavior (v. 13). First, Paul explains what type of behavior is improper for believers. The negatives he lists illustrate three characteristics that are not to mark a Christian's lifestyle. The first trait is a *lack of personal discipline.* Christians are not to use their leisure time as an opportunity for engaging in wrongful activities. That is what Paul means by the word *carousing.* Furthermore, we should not allow alcohol or any other drug to so control us that a state of "drunkenness" characterizes our lives. The second quality Paul mentions is a *lack of personal morality.* Christians are forbidden from engaging "in sexual promiscuity and sensuality." Although our society permits and promotes such practices, the Lord does not want us to fall prey to these traps. The third trait of a darkened lifestyle is a *lack of love in personal relationships.* Christians are told to keep "strife and jealousy" out of their associations with others.

B. Proper Provision (v. 14). Next, Paul explains how we should live. His counsel is twofold. Positively, we need to "put on the Lord Jesus Christ." By drawing on His strength, aligning our thoughts with His mind-set, and yielding our wills to His revealed plan, we can live as beacons in the midst of darkness. Negatively, we should "make no provision for the flesh in regard to its lusts." We all find that certain people, places, activities, or situations promote sin in our lives. Knowing this, we should do whatever is possible to avoid them. But when we cannot remove ourselves from their sphere of influence, then we need to draw upon the sufficient provisions granted to us by Christ. For only through Him can we overcome the temptations that threaten to overtake us.

IV. Our Minds Recall.

In one sentence we can wrap up the many thoughts presented here: *We are not alone; Christ is with us, and He will never leave us.* We can begin each day secure in the fact that He sees, hears, and knows what we do. And we can be thankful that daily He reproves our sins, forgives our failures, strengthens us when we are weak, and urges us to reflect His light in a spiritually dark world. So let's wake up and move out as beacons into the night before the dawn breaks with Christ's return.

Living Insights

Study One

This thirteenth chapter of Romans is rich in valuable concepts for the child of God. We can gain a greater appreciation of its worth by discovering the meanings of its key words.

- Make a copy of this chart in your notebook, then reread Romans 13:1–14. Write down the words you consider to be significant. Once you have done this, seek to define each term by first checking the context. If the context does not give you the clues you need, then consult a good Bible dictionary.

Romans 13:1–14		
Key Words	Verses	Definitions

Living Insights

Study Two

"But put on the Lord Jesus Christ, and make no provision for the flesh in regard to its lusts" (Rom. 13:14). Let's break down this verse by asking some probing, personal questions.

- How do *you* "put on the Lord Jesus Christ"?
- How do *you* "make no provision for the flesh"?
- How do *you* deal with your "lusts"?

Taboo or Not Taboo?

Romans 14:1–12

Various people are offended by different things. For example, some persons are quite adamant in their view that Christianity and alcohol just don't mix. Others, however, do not struggle with a believer drinking an alcoholic beverage on occasion. Certain individuals become upset when they see a Christian woman wearing makeup, while others have no problem accepting this custom. Instances such as these are not new in church history. The New Testament records several situations wherein Christian parties adopted opposing stances on certain practices. Unfortunately, too many of these instances resulted in selfish feuds rather than selfless love-acts. How should believers who strongly disagree on nonessential issues relate to one another? The answer is found in Romans 14:1–12. Let's pay close attention, for the unity of the church both locally and universally depends on our adherence to the counsel presented in these verses.

I. The Background.

In order to clearly grasp the principles taught in this text, we need to gain some knowledge concerning its historical setting.

A. Certain Actions. Among the Roman Christians Paul addresses, some were creating waves of disharmony because of their disagreements over certain practices. One point of contention arose between those believers who held that "all things" were permissible to eat and those who thought that only "vegetables" were allowable (v. 2). Although Paul does not specify it here, the issue probably concerned meat sacrificed to idols (cf. 1 Cor. 8). It was customary in Paul's day for the Greek and Roman pagans to burn in their sacrifices the less desirable portions of an animal while saving the choicer sections for personal consumption and sale to the public. Occasionally, the market where this meat could be bought was located adjacent to, or inside of, a temple designed for idol worship. Therefore, in the minds of many, there was such a close association between the sacrificial meat and idolatry that even to purchase it suggested involvement in pagan religious practices. Another action that created division among the Roman believers concerned an individual's response toward certain days. Some Christians regarded "one day above another," while others treated "every day alike" (Rom. 14:5). Again, though Paul does not tell us, perhaps one of the days in question was Saturday—the Jewish Sabbath. Christians who had come from a strong Jewish background may have still regarded Saturday as a sacred day of rest. If so, then they probably would have been offended by other Christians who did not view Saturday as possessing any special significance.

B. Critical Reactions. It is not difficult to imagine the heated friction that must have arisen between the opposing sides on these questions. In fact, Paul informs us that there were two critical responses. The first one concerned those who were "weak in faith" (v. 1). These were the scrupulous Christians who adhered to a rigid view about diet and days. These weak believers stood guilty of judging those who both ate sacrificial meat and failed to observe special days. The second reaction came from those believers who were strong in their faith (vv. 1–2; cf. Rom. 15:1). These libertarian Christians viewed their weaker brethren with contempt (Rom. 14:3).

II. The Groups.

We may discern from Romans that of the two groups, Paul stood theologically on the side of the strong Christians. For in opposition to the believers who thought that certain foods were unclean, Paul proclaimed, "I know and am convinced in the Lord Jesus that nothing is unclean in itself; but to him who thinks anything to be unclean, to him it is unclean" (Rom. 14:14; cf. 1 Cor. 8:4–13). Paul also included himself among the strong in faith when he wrote, "Now we who are strong ought to bear the weaknesses of those without strength and not just please ourselves" (Rom. 15:1). He knew that the doctrinal teaching of Scripture favored the position of the Christian libertarians. But he also realized that the deeper issue was not theological but attitudinal. The crucial problem that needed to be addressed was the critical responses of the groups to one another.

III. The Attitudes.

Paul says that the strong believers treated their weaker brethren with *contempt* (Rom. 14:3a). The Greek term for this word means "to regard as nothing, to utterly despise." The libertarian Christians were acting superior to the more scrupulous ones. Rather than exercising their biblical freedom discreetly and responsibly, they were flaunting it in the faces of those who could not handle it. As such, they were entirely discounting the feelings and beliefs of the weaker group. The narrow-minded believers, on the other hand, also displayed a faulty attitude. They became *judgmental* of the more liberal Christians (v. 3b). Rather than broaden their understanding of freedom in Christ, they adopted a view of condemnation toward those who ate the wrong foods and treated every day alike.

IV. The Principles.

Throughout Romans 14:1–12, Paul sets forth several principles that we would be wise to recall and apply. These timeless guidelines show how two parties who disagree on the *nonessentials* of the Christian faith can live in harmony.

An Important Note

Whenever Christians find that they have disagreements over the *essential* truths of Christianity—such as Christ's deity, His virgin birth, the substitutionary atonement, His bodily Resurrection, His Second Coming, and the infallible authority of Scripture—then the issues must be resolved by an appeal to the clear teaching of the Bible. Serious questions regarding the foundational doctrines of the faith cannot be left unresolved without bringing detrimental consequences to the individuals directly and indirectly involved.

A. **The stronger Christians should accept the weaker ones** (v. 1). We are to freely embrace those who hold differing opinions. And we should not bring with our acceptance a hidden agenda to change their views so that they coincide with ours.
B. **Christians should realize that God accepts both strong and weak believers** (v. 3). Therefore, we should be just as committed to one another as the Lord is to us.
C. **All Christians are under the same Head** (vv. 4, 8–9). Because we are all servants of one Master, we do not have the authority to judge other believers. Only the Lord has the right, knowledge, and wisdom to accurately evaluate the opinions and practices of His people. After all, He is our Owner; we neither own Him nor one another. Therefore, our ultimate accountability is to Christ, not to other Christians.
D. **Christians should be fully convinced of their stand** (v. 5b). We should be as certain as possible that whatever position we might maintain on nonessential issues is in accord with what we feel the Lord would have us do. For "happy is he who does not condemn himself in what he approves. But he who doubts is condemned if he eats, because his eating is not from faith; and whatever is not from faith is sin" (vv. 22b–23).
E. **All Christians are interrelated** (v. 7). As the verse states, "For not one of us lives for himself, and not one dies for himself." Because we are linked together in the bond of Christ, our actions affect each other. Therefore, we should seek to support one another rather than use our energy to tear each other down.
F. **All Christians will face the same Judge** (vv. 10–12). "We shall all stand before the judgment seat of God." At that time, "each one of us shall give account of himself to God." Thus, there is no good reason for weak believers to pass judgment on the strong or for strong believers to contemptuously disregard the weak. The righteous Lord of all will one day impartially judge the thoughts, motives, actions, and beliefs of all Christians. That fact should humble us in our dealings with one another.

Living Insights

Study One

There are quite a few pronouns in this passage. It would be helpful to our understanding of the text if we clarified the key ones.

- In Romans 14:1–12, look for the words *he, his, him, you, us,* and *we.* After writing them in your copy of this chart, go back to the text in order to determine whom each pronoun refers to. Place your answers in the right column.

Romans 14:1–12		
Pronouns	Verses	To Whom the Pronouns Refer
He		
His		
Him		
You		
Us		
We		

Living Insights

Study Two

Maybe it's difficult for you to imagine churches splitting over the practices of eating meat or resting on Saturday. Perhaps those are taboos that are foreign to your particular circle of Christianity. But more than likely, there are other points of disagreement among the believers you associate with. For our purposes here, let's take our eyes off others and place them on ourselves. The exercises given below will help you to do exactly that!

- Get together with someone who knows you well. Ask them the following questions about how they perceive your taboos. Be prepared; some things may be said that are hard to hear. So ask God for strength, wisdom, and discernment in your responses.
  - —What do you perceive to be my personal taboos?
  - —How do I seem to handle people with whom I disagree?
  - —Do you view me as a strong or weak believer?
  - —How would you assess my relationships with other Christians?

Liberty on a Tightrope

Romans 14:13–23

Balance . . . that's the name of the game. And one of our enemies in the contest is the expert of extremes. Satan will do anything he can to move us off center and into an imbalanced lifestyle. Take Christian liberty as an example. God's desire is that we fully enjoy our freedom in Christ. And yet without self-imposed limits, we risk becoming selfish islands and careless rebels who have little regard for others. Romans 14 takes us to the heart of this issue and exposes our motives—the tender nerves that prompt our actions. What we will learn is that we must exercise our freedom with the discretion that flows from genuine love.

I. The Correct Stance to Start With.

As believers in Christ, we walk the tightrope of liberty. On either side of us lie two extremes—legalism and license. The first one threatens to place us under a strict, narrow set of rules and regulations. The second urges us toward the bondage of self-centeredness and immorality. Somehow, we need to avoid these extremes. How can we do it? The answer is found in these words: "Therefore let us not judge one another anymore, but rather determine this—not to put an obstacle or a stumbling block in a brother's way" (Rom. 14:13). Paul is exhorting us not to judge others but to assess ourselves. In addition, he calls on us to exercise freedom with our brethren's welfare in mind. Put another way, *we can successfully traverse the tightrope of liberty when we seek a proper balance between self-control and a love for others.* Now we should note that the context of this counsel does not concern legalists, but it does focus on how stronger Christians ought to treat weaker ones. Believers who are weak in the faith, although they may be open to growth, are spiritually immature. Legalists, on the other hand, are also spiritual babes, but they stubbornly refuse to mature in Christian liberty. This type of individual was challenged theologically in the Book of Galatians. There Paul exhorted believers to remain free from the shackles of legalism (Gal. 5:1). Yet, in the same letter, he urged Christians not to turn their "freedom into an opportunity for the flesh, but through love serve one another" (v. 13b). In summary, then, the key to a balanced Christian life lies neither in legalism, for that destroys freedom, nor in license, for that abuses freedom. Rather, balance in one's life and unity in Christ's Church can only be achieved through the responsible exercise of one's liberty.

II. Three Principles for Maintaining Balance.

In Romans 14:14–20, we discover some guidelines that provide the direction we need for the proper use of our Christian freedom. Let's seek to grasp each one as it appears in the text.

A. **Nothing is intrinsically unclean** (vv. 14–16). With full confidence Paul states, "I know and am convinced in the Lord Jesus that nothing is unclean in itself" (v. 14a). When God created the universe, He declared that all He had made was "very good" (Gen. 1:31a). And although the Fall of man has brought God's creation under a curse (Gen. 3, Rom. 8:19–23), it has not altered the essential goodness of what God has made. This truth is affirmed by Paul in these words: "For everything created by God *is* good, and nothing is to be rejected, if it is received with gratitude" (1 Tim. 4:4, emphasis added). Therefore, there is no biblical basis for regarding some aspects of the creation as evil. All things were created good, and they are still good in themselves. On this foundational truth rests Christian freedom. However, not every Christian has accepted this fact. Some believers think that certain things are "unclean." Whatever they regard as unclean is so in their minds even though it is good in reality (Rom. 14:14b). Thus, when a Christian engages in an essentially good activity before other Christians who perceive it as wrong, he is running the risk of seriously hurting their walk with God. Because of this, believers should limit the expressions of their liberty out of love for the weaker brethren (vv. 15–16). Such a love-act does not deny the principle that everything in creation is intrinsically good. Rather, it flows from the recognition of the fact that a fellow believer's growth in Christ is more important than the full exercise of one's freedom.

B. **The essence of Christianity is not found in externals** (vv. 17–19). This second principle of liberty is manifested quite clearly in these words from Paul: "For the kingdom of God is not eating and drinking, but righteousness and peace and joy in the Holy Spirit" (v. 17). Whatever we do should promote these traits in others. If our actions before certain individuals will not encourage such qualities, then we should refrain from performing them around those people. When our Christian freedom is exercised with this level of maturity and wisdom, we will find our behavior "acceptable to God and approved by men" (v. 18). "So then," Paul concludes, "let us pursue the things which make for peace and the building up of one another" (v. 19).

C. **When the exercise of Christian liberty threatens to hinder God's work, it should be restrained** (v. 20). As Paul says, "Do not tear down the work of God for the sake of food. All things indeed are clean, but they are evil for the man who eats and gives offense." Because God's creation is essentially good, we have every right to enjoy it to the fullest measure.

However, we should keep our right from becoming a stumbling block to those who are less mature in the faith. Love commands that we limit our liberty, when necessary, for the sake of others.

III. Essential Ways for Guarding against Stumbling.

What are some steps we can take that will help keep other believers from stumbling over us? Paul gives three practical applications.

A. Be considerate (v. 21). When we are in the company of another Christian who regards certain good things as evil, we should care enough to avoid those things.

B. Be convinced (v. 22a). If we are engaged in certain activities that are not clearly prohibited by the teaching of Scripture, then we should be confident in our thinking that they are right. If we entertain any doubts about the goodness of these actions, then we should give them up.

C. Be consistent (vv. 22b–23). When we arrive at the conclusion that something is right, unless we receive solid confirmation to the contrary, we should not waver in our conviction. For doubts concerning our beliefs will yield internal condemnation, but consistency in belief will bring us happiness.

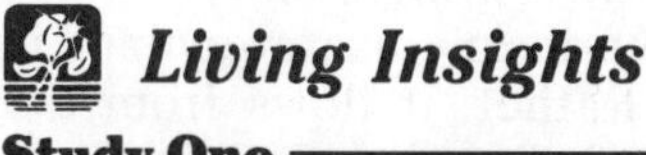

Study One

The Magna Charta of Christian liberty is stated in the Book of Galatians. This letter gives us the balance we need for walking the tightrope of liberty.

- How well do you understand your liberty? Using a copy of this chart as a guide, carefully read through Galatians and make notes of your observations concerning Christian liberty.

Galatians: Liberty Observed	
Observations	Verses

Living Insights

Study Two

Let's get to the heart of the issue. Have you been guilty of causing a brother to stumble? Isn't it time to make things right?

- If you have caused a fellow Christian to stumble, contact him or her and arrange to get together. Use your meeting as a chance to demonstrate the love, consideration, and control we've been studying about. Strive for a meaningful occasion of restoration.
- If you search your conscience and find you've not caused anyone to stumble, spend this time in prayer. Ask God to help keep you from becoming a stumbling block to others.

We Are One . . . or Are We?

Romans 15:1–13

The day before Jesus was crucified, He made the following request of His Father on behalf of all Christians: " 'That they may all be one; even as Thou, Father, art in Me, and I in Thee, that they also may be in Us; that the world may believe that Thou didst send Me. And the glory which Thou hast given Me I have given to them; that they may be one, just as We are one; . . . that they may be perfected in unity' " (John 17:21–23a). Three times in these verses Jesus emphasizes the importance He places on the oneness of all believers. Indeed, He bases His strategy for evangelism on the unity of His Body, the Church. Are we, as the familiar song declares, "one in the bond of love"? Or are we selfishly seeking to fulfill our individual dreams and promote our personal opinions? These are tough questions; they demand soul-searching answers. Let's keep these inquiries before us as we dig our way through Romans 15:1–13. For in this passage Paul highlights the essentials involved in cultivating a harmonious unity within the ranks of Christianity.

I. For the Sake of God's Work.

From what Paul said in chapter 14, we may conclude that the makings for a church split were present in the Roman church. The main issues of dispute concerned diet and days. Some Christians thought that they were free in Christ to eat anything, while others believed that vegetables were the only food permissible to consume (Rom. 14:2). Furthermore, certain believers maintained that some days had special religious significance, while other Christians treated every day alike (v. 5). The problem did not lie in the fact that there were differences of opinion over such nonessential subjects. Rather, it was the attitudes and actions of those who held the opposing opinions that threatened the church's unity. The stronger Christians were contemptuously flaunting their freedom before the weaker believers. On the other side, the immature Christians were snubly judging the beliefs and behavior of the mature believers in their midst. In short, neither group was exercising authentic love toward the other. Consequently, their infighting seriously threatened to divide the Roman church. Realizing this, Paul urged them to be considerate toward one another (v. 21), convinced that their opinions and actions were right for them (v. 22a), and consistent in the outworking of their beliefs (vv. 22b–23).

II. Among God's People.

When two or more believers gather together, we should realize that not only is Christ in their midst (Matt. 18:20), but differences in temperament, background, conviction, belief, and spiritual maturity also exist. So how can the Lord's people keep their differences from destroying their unity? Put more positively, what can Christians do to perpetuate harmony without sacrificing variety of expression in nonessential matters? Besides applying the counsel given in Romans 14, we can accomplish this goal by heeding the wisdom presented in the first several verses of chapter 15. So let's seek to discover the pearls hidden there.

A. An Obligation (vv. 1–2). This passage tells us that "we who are strong ought to bear the weaknesses of those without strength and not just please ourselves. Let each of us please his neighbor for his good, to his edification." Rather than being self-centered, God exhorts us to be other-centered. How can we fulfill this injunction? We can do so by both bearing each other's burdens (cf. Gal. 6:2) and seeking to build each other up. This counsel strikes right at the heart of selfishness—the central threat of Christian unity.

B. An Illustration (v. 3). The ultimate example of an other-oriented lifestyle is Jesus Christ. As verse 3 states, "For even Christ did not please Himself; but as it is written, 'The reproaches of those who reproached Thee fell upon me' " (cf. Ps. 69:9). In the timeless realm of heaven, the Son of God enjoyed unending bliss, majestic glory, and unbroken fellowship with His Father. However, when He descended to earth and "became flesh" (John 1:14a), He opened Himself up to heartache, frustration, pain, and even death. Why? Certainly not for His own pleasure. While facing impending crucifixion, Jesus prayed, " 'Father, if Thou art willing, remove this cup from Me; yet not My will, but Thine be done' " (Luke 22:42). His ultimate goal was to please God the Father even if it entailed intense personal agony and humiliation (Luke 22:44, 63–65; 23:10–46).

C. Some Motivation (v. 4). Paul referred to Psalm 69 in Romans 15:3 and applied it to the selflessness of Christ. Apparently, his use of this text brought to his mind how the Old Testament can aid believers in their walk with God. Thus, Paul pointed out that the Old Testament books were "written for our instruction, that through perseverance and the encouragement of the Scriptures we might have hope." These inspired documents are replete with accounts of godly men and women who lived above their circumstances by riveting their eyes on God while ministering to the people around them. In other words, the Old Testament is a great source of motivation for those who need encouragement in serving others rather than themselves.

D. Some Application (vv. 5–7). In these verses Paul prays that the divine Author of the Scriptures would give His people the "perseverance and encouragement . . . to be of the same mind with one another according to Christ Jesus" (v. 5). This does not mean that Christians are to think, feel, look, and act alike. Rather, it means that believers are to have the same focal point for their lives—namely, Jesus Christ. With Him as their referent, they will be able to unite "with one voice [to] glorify the God and Father of our Lord Jesus Christ" (v. 6). So the divine aspect of Paul's application is that God works to promote and preserve our unity. The human side, however, is that we work to "accept one another, just as Christ also accepted us to the glory of God" (v. 7). Jesus died for us when we were ungodly sinners—rebels against God (Rom. 5:6–11). If He could accept us when we were in such a wicked state, then how much more should we seek to accept all believers—even those who disagree with us on incidental matters.

III. Consider God's Son.

Paul drives his message home by telling us what role Christ has played in laying the foundation for Christian unity. He says that the Lord "has become a servant to the circumcision"—that is, the Jews—and "the Gentiles," who are non-Jews (vv. 8–9a). No two groups could be more opposite than these. By Christ's day, many Jews had become legalists who still maintained a rigorous belief in one God. The Gentiles, on the other hand, were often morally loose individuals who believed in the existence of many gods. One of the few commonalities between these diverse groups was the animosity they had toward one another. And yet, the Son of God came to serve both Jews and Gentiles by uniting them under the common bond of the Christian faith. The broad acceptance demonstrated by Christ should also be manifested by those of us who are His by divine grace.

IV. Because of God's Power.

Paul wraps up his counsel with the following benediction: "Now may the God of hope fill you with all joy and peace in believing, that you may abound in hope by the power of the Holy Spirit" (v. 13). Integral to the maximal experience of joy, peace, and hope is Christian unity. Without harmony among the believers in a local assembly, there can be few expressions of abiding joy, corporate peace, or lasting hope. Of course, it is humanly impossible to achieve the oneness Paul has spoken about. But then again, we are serving a God who specializes in accomplishing the humanly impossible (Matt. 19:26). So let's begin accepting one another in the way He has commanded, all the while depending on Him to empower our efforts toward the goal of unity.

Living Insights

Study One

Did you understand everything you read in Romans 15:1–13? There may have been some things that you struggled with. So let's do some digging!

- Copy the following chart into your notebook. Read through Romans 15:1–13 and answer from the text the questions listed below. If you need additional assistance, consult a good Bible commentary.

Romans 15:1–13	
Questions	Answers
Who?	
What?	
Where?	
When?	
Why?	
How?	

Living Insights

Study Two

Unity is a great theme of the faith. One proof of that fact is the abundance of marvelous hymns and gospel songs that speak of our oneness.

- Let's use this time to sing praises to God for our unity. Dust off the hymnal and look for songs that give at least a portion of their lyrics to the theme of harmony. You may choose to sing with others or perhaps opt to quietly meditate on the lyrics alone. Either way, make this a grand time of worship!

Competent Christians

Romans 15:14–16

Most New Testament scholars believe that Paul concludes his major thoughts to the Roman Christians in the thirteenth verse of chapter 15. This being so, the remainder of the letter forms an epilogue of some important personal remarks. A studious reading of this closing section certainly supports their opinion. In the three verses that open the epilogue, we will hear Paul give his assessment of the believers who comprised the first-century church at Rome. We will also learn the main reason Paul wrote this letter to them in such bold terms. Although what he says was written long ago, it speaks with ringing relevance to us today.

I. The Epilogue Explained.

The closing section of Romans falls neatly into six divisions. Becoming familiar with them will help us to get a better handle on its content. The first part is contained in chapter 15, verses 14–16, and it focuses on the *Roman Christians.* The next division encompasses verses 17–29. There the *Apostle Paul* zeros in on himself. The last four verses of chapter 15 make up the third part, and they are concerned with a *prayer request* from Paul. A lengthy list of *personal greetings* is found in the first sixteen verses of chapter 16. They compose the fourth section of the epilogue. Paul delivers a *final warning* to the Roman Christians in the fifth division, and it may be found in chapter 16, verses 17–24. In the final three verses of the letter, Paul gives a *closing benediction* that comprises the sixth part of the epilogue.

II. The Church Exposed.

In this lesson we will set our sights on the first few verses of the epilogue. There we learn that Paul has some compliments to pay his Roman readers. It is not the first time that he has commended them in the letter. Back in chapter 1, he positively commented on their evangelistic zeal: "I thank my God through Jesus Christ for you all, because your faith is being proclaimed throughout the whole world" (Rom. 1:8). Now toward the end of his letter, he again encourages them by highlighting some more of their strengths.

A. Inwardly Good. Paul compliments this characteristic in these words: "And concerning you, my brethren, I myself also am convinced that you yourselves are full of goodness" (Rom. 15:14a). The Apostle is not asserting here that his readers were sinless. He knew that they, along with all other living Christians, were still in the process of being set free from sin's power. Rather, the phrase "full of goodness" conveys the idea that these first-century believers were characterized by moral excellence in their lifestyles. They strove to do what was right.

This demonstrated that they were actively yielding to the Holy Spirit's sanctifying work in their lives.

B. **Well Informed.** Paul goes on to say that the Roman Christians were "filled with all knowledge" (v. 14b). This does not mean that they were omniscient. However, it does mean that they were faithful in executing the truth they had received. They applied what they knew about Christianity instead of letting it collect dust in their minds and on their notepads.

C. **Deeply Caring.** The believers in Rome were also complimented for their ability "to admonish one another" (v. 14c). The Greek term translated *admonish* comes from two other words—one that means "mind" and another which means "to put something somewhere." When these words are combined to form the term *admonish,* they convey the idea of "placing something in the mind." One New Testament scholar communicates the fuller meaning of the word in this way: "It is an appeal to the mind where opposition is present. The person is led away from a false way through warning, instruction, reminding, teaching, and encouraging and his conduct is to be corrected."* In other words, the Roman Christians cared so deeply about one another that they took the time and the risk to lovingly confront those in their midst who were veering off the right path. Many of us fail to handle conflicts as they did. Indeed, we often opt for other alternatives, such as (1) avoiding the confrontation altogether, (2) facing it head-on but with a prideful attitude, or (3) acknowledging the problem but shrugging it off for the sake of maintaining friendship or harmony. However, none of these responses are right. If we truly love someone, then we will care enough to express our love through confrontation no matter how painful it may be. As Proverbs 27:6 states, "Faithful are the wounds of a friend, but deceitful are the kisses of an enemy."

D. **Missionary Heart.** This fourth commendable trait is stated by Paul in the form of a reminder. Notice what he says: "But I have written very boldly to you on some points, so as to remind you again, because of the grace that was given me from God, to be a minister of Christ Jesus to the Gentiles" (vv. 15–16a). The basic meaning of the Greek word for *Gentiles* is "nations"—namely, all non-Jewish peoples. Paul reiterates to the Roman believers that their evangelistic enthusiasm should be concentrated not only on the Jews but also on the other peoples

*Fritz Rienecker, *A Linguistic Key to the Greek New Testament,* edited by Cleon L. Rogers, Jr. (Grand Rapids: Zondervan Publishing House, 1980), p. 382.

of the world (cf. Rom. 1:16). And since Rome was an international crossroad of travel and commerce, these Christians had the world at their doorstep. By reaching out to those who lived, studied, and worked in their city, they could have an impact for the gospel that was far-reaching indeed.

E. Disciple Makers. To this reminder Paul added that the Roman believers minister as priests "the gospel of God, [so] that my offering of the Gentiles might become acceptable, sanctified by the Holy Spirit" (v. 16b). A priest, or servant, is concerned not only with one's conversion but also with one's sanctification. When we serve others as priests of the gospel, we become involved in its every facet. Among its many aspects, three are central: proclaiming freedom from the penalty of sin (justification), helping others with their release from the power of sin (sanctification), and encouraging believers with the hope of their final deliverance from the very presence of sin (glorification). In other words, like the early Roman Christians, we are to be both spiritual obstetricians and pediatricians. We should be servants who help unbelievers become born again into the family of God as well as disciple them through the growing-up process.

III. The Believer Exhorted.

As we review the compliments conveyed in these verses, we can see that they contain two lines of thought. One refers to ourselves as individuals, and the other concerns ourselves as ministers. When we put these two major areas together, we discover that Paul has set forth five key traits of a *competent Christian.* Let's take a few moments to do some self-evaluation. To facilitate this, let's personalize the following application. Without comparing yourself to other people, seek to honestly answer the questions given below.

A. Regarding Myself. Is my focus on doing what is right? Am I cooperating with the Holy Spirit's work in my life, or am I fighting it by continuing to yield to sinful habits? Am I striving to apply my knowledge of Christian truth? If not, then why? Do I care enough to lovingly confront others?

B. Regarding My Ministry. Do I have a desire to see others come to Christ? Am I reaching out with the gospel, or am I keeping the message to myself? Am I encouraging other believers to flesh out Christianity more consistently? Am I providing them with a good example to follow?

Living Insights

Study One

Isn't the Word of God wonderfully practical? These final chapters of Romans serve as fabulous examples of God speaking to us today! Let's take a few moments to plummet the depths of one of these chapters.

- First locate a version of the Bible that you usually don't use. It may be a translation or a paraphrase; either one is fine. Then carefully, and preferably aloud, read Romans 15. You'll be pleasantly surprised at how much more meaning you can discover just by reading the passage in a different version.

Living Insights

Study Two

Are you a competent Christian? Paul gives us five characteristics of one in Romans 15:14–16. You can test your level of competency by taking the brief quiz that follows. Circle the number under each trait that describes your level of competency (10 meaning best, 1 meaning worst). Finally, think through the results of this evaluation, then commit yourself to a game plan that is designed to help bring about improvement.

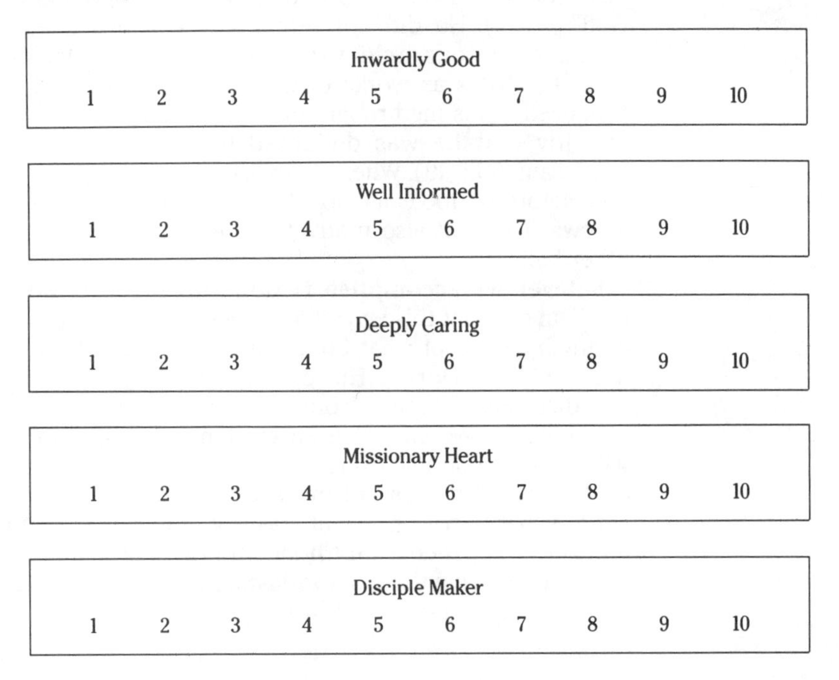

Inwardly Good

1 2 3 4 5 6 7 8 9 10

Well Informed

1 2 3 4 5 6 7 8 9 10

Deeply Caring

1 2 3 4 5 6 7 8 9 10

Missionary Heart

1 2 3 4 5 6 7 8 9 10

Disciple Maker

1 2 3 4 5 6 7 8 9 10

Preaching and Truckin'

Romans 15:17–29

Although the Apostle Paul was one of the greatest men who ever lived, he seldom wrote much about himself in his letters. Fortunately, the epilogue of Romans stands as a marked exception. There he allows us an opportunity to peer into the deep recesses of his mind. This is especially true in the following verses we are going to cover. So let's approach this autobiographical passage with the expectation that we can learn much from the life of a person who was deeply committed to God.

I. Paul's Philosophy.

The first snapshot Paul gives concerns two main aspects of his philosophy of life. They may be found in verses 17–21 of Romans 15. Let's consider them carefully.

A. Regarding Accomplishments—A Servant (vv. 17–19). As an active missionary, Paul had many achievements. What was his perspective on them? How did he regard his accomplishments? This text suggests three statements that adequately answer these questions.

1. **Accomplishments bring a sense of personal satisfaction.** Paul could say, "Therefore in Christ Jesus I have found reason for boasting in things pertaining to God" (v. 17). He did not refuse any acknowledgement of his numerous achievements. Indeed, he declared them to others as works of God. The victories God had produced in his life brought him an inner sense of reward and joy that he was delighted to share with others (cf. 2 Sam. 6:12–19). When we experience accomplishment and victory, we too can enjoy the sense of achievement that follows. This will also motivate us to share our joy with other believers.
2. **Whatever we accomplish is done through us, not by us.** Paul stated it this way: "For I will not presume to speak of anything except what Christ has accomplished through me" (v. 18a). During His earthly ministry, Jesus told His disciples, " 'Apart from Me you can do nothing' " (John 15:5b). We cannot even exist moment by moment without the continual exercise of Christ's sustaining power (Col. 1:17). This does not mean that Christ performs our actions, but it does mean at least two things: (1) that we are totally dependent on Christ, and (2) that if we desire to accomplish anything of everlasting worth, then we must do it in cooperation with Christ.

3. **All genuine accomplishments are actual, not imaginary.** When Paul looked back upon his life, he could point to individuals who had been saved as a result of his words and deeds (vv. 18b–19). In fact, the people he had touched were so spread throughout the Mediterranean area that he could say, "From Jerusalem and round about as far as Illyricum I have fully preached the gospel of Christ" (v. 19b). By making this statement, Paul displayed neither an inflated opinion of himself nor a false sense of humility. Rather, he knew that he could provide specific examples of what Christ had accomplished through his service. We should be able to do the same if the Lord is really working through us.

B. Regarding Ministry—A Pioneer (vv. 20–21). If you look on a Bible map of the New Testament era, you will find that the region of Illyricum was northwest of Jerusalem and just east of Italy and the Adriatic Sea. Paul said that by the time he was finishing his letter to the Romans, he had already "fully preached the gospel of Christ" in the areas between Jerusalem and Illyricum (v. 19b). If Paul had been referring to the United States, he could have communicated the same idea by stating that he had preached from Miami, Florida to Seattle, Washington. What motivated him to take the good news about Christ to so many regions? In verses 20–21, he told us: "And thus I aspired to preach the gospel, not where Christ was already named, that I might not build upon another man's foundation; but as it is written, 'They who had no news of Him shall see, and they who have not heard shall understand.' " Because he did not want to reevangelize areas, he pioneered unreached regions for the cause of Christ. He wanted to give those who had never heard the gospel message an opportunity for new life. Thus, his vision was as big as the world he knew. Indeed, as we will learn in just a moment, he wanted to take the good news to the farthest corner of the then known world—Spain. Unlike many of us, Paul was not guilty of dreaming too small. He knew that he served a great God who could do great things through him if he would be at God's disposal.

II. Paul's Itinerary.

In verses 23–28, Paul laid out his traveling plans for the believers in Rome. His words reveal both a pioneer spirit and a servant's heart.

A. To Jerusalem (vv. 25–27). This was the first destination on Paul's itinerary. Jerusalem was the birthplace of Christianity. It was there that Christ died on the cross and rose from the dead. This city also witnessed the beginnings of Christ's Church

(Acts 1:8, 12; 2:1–47). However, since those days, tough times had fallen on the Christians who lived there. So Paul had taken the opportunity in his travels to gather some financial support for "the poor among the saints in Jerusalem" (Rom. 15:26b). The contributions came from believers in Macedonia and Achaia (v. 26a). Paul noted that they were pleased to help financially (vv. 26a, 27a). But he mentioned that even if they did not desire to help the Christians in Jerusalem, they would still be obligated to do so since they were spiritually indebted to them (v. 27b). In other words, spiritual blessing breeds material obligation. If we have been aided in our walk with God by someone, then we should serve that individual by giving of our material possessions when he or she is in need. Of course, this is not the only way in which we can express our appreciation to others, but it is certainly a biblical expectation.

B. To Rome (vv. 23–24). Here Paul conveyed his intention to finally make it to Rome—the capitol of the Roman Empire. Why had he longed for so many years to see the believers in that city? There were two reasons. First, Paul just wanted to enjoy their company for a while (v. 24b). He reveled in the thought of having a delightful visit with the Roman believers whom he had not seen. Second, Paul wanted to receive from them some financial aid for his trip to Spain (v. 24a). He was depending on them to demonstrate their appreciation for spiritual renewal by materially giving to the further spreading of the gospel.

C. To Spain (vv. 24, 28). This was the final geographic destination of Paul. New Testament scholars disagree on whether he ever made it that far west. But the following excerpt from a letter by a first-century Roman Christian named Clement suggests that Paul did finally minister in Spain:

> After that he [Paul] had been seven times in bonds, had been driven into exile, had been stoned, had preached in the East and in the West, he won the noble renown which was the reward of his faith, having taught righteousness unto the *whole world* and having reached the *farthest bounds of the West* [Spain]; and when he had borne his testimony before the rulers [those in Rome], so he departed from the world. (emphasis added)*

*Clement of Rome, *I Clement* 5. Cited from Richard N. Longenecker's book *The Ministry and Message of Paul* (Grand Rapids: Zondervan Publishing House, 1971), p. 85.

Insight for Living
Cassette Tapes
Relating to Others in Love

The final five chapters of Romans make the Christian aware of the all-important role of love—authentic love, demonstrative love, the kind of love that makes Christianity magnetic. Here are sixteen messages that open our understanding of Romans 12–16 and challenge us to relate to others in love.

U.S.	**Cassette series—includes album cover**	**$44.50**
ROL CS	**Individual cassettes—include messages A and B**	**5.00**
Canadian	**Cassette series—includes album cover**	**$56.50**
ROL CS	**Individual cassettes—include messages A and B**	**6.35**

These prices are effective as of August 1985 and are subject to change.

ROL 1-A: ***How Faith Functions***
Romans 12:1–8
B: ***Love Exposed***
Romans 12:9–13

ROL 2-A: ***You and Your Enemy***
Romans 12:14–21
B: ***How to Be a Godly Rebel***
Romans 13:1–7

ROL 3-A: ***Legal Tender and Loving Care***
Romans 13:8–10
B: ***Wake Up and Get Dressed!***
Romans 13:11–14

ROL 4-A: ***Taboo or Not Taboo?***
Romans 14:1–12
B: ***Liberty on a Tightrope***
Romans 14:13–23

ROL 5-A: ***We Are One . . . or Are We?***
Romans 15:1–13
B: ***Competent Christians***
Romans 15:14–16

ROL 6-A: ***Preaching and Truckin'***
Romans 15:17–29
B: ***How to Make Prayer Practical***
Acts 12:1–16, Romans 15:30–33

ROL 7-A: ***You May Kiss the Bride***
Romans 16:1–16
B: ***When Trouble Is Brewing***
Romans 16:17–20

ROL 8-A: ***Unseen Evil and Uplifting Good***
Romans 16:17–24
B: ***To God Be the Glory Forever***
Romans 16:25–27

Additional Ordering Information

Payment Options: We accept personal checks, money orders, Visa, and MasterCard in payment for materials ordered. Unfortunately, we are unable to offer invoicing or COD orders. If the amount of your check or money order is less than the amount of your purchase, your check will be returned so that you may place your order again with the correct amount. All orders must be paid in full before shipment can be made.

U.S. Ordering Information: You are welcome to use our toll-free number (for orders only) between the hours of 8:30 A.M. and 4:00 P.M., Pacific Time. We can accept only Visa or MasterCard when ordering by phone. The number is (800) 772-8888. This number may be used anywhere in the continental United States excluding California, Hawaii, and Alaska. Orders from those areas are handled through our Sales Department at (714) 870-9161. We are unable to accept collect calls.

Your order will be processed promptly. We ask that you allow four to six weeks for delivery by fourth-class mail. If you wish your order to be shipped first-class, please add 10 percent of the total order (not including California sales tax) for shipping and handling.

Canadian Ordering Information: Your order will be processed promptly. We ask that you allow approximately four weeks for delivery by first-class mail to the U.S./Canadian border. All orders will be shipped from our office in Fullerton, California. For our listeners in British Columbia, a 7 percent sales tax must be added to the total of all tape orders (not including first-class postage). For further information, please contact our office at (604) 669-1916.

Returned Checks: There is a $10 charge for any returned check (regardless of the amount of your order) to cover processing and invoicing.

Guarantee: Our tapes are guaranteed for ninety days from the date of shipping against faulty performance or breakage due to a defect in the tape. For best results, please be sure your tape recorder is in good operating condition and is cleaned regularly.

Quantity Discounts and Gift Certificates Are Available upon Request

Order Form

Please send me the following cassette tapes:

The current series: ☐ ROL CS Relating to Others in Love

Individual tapes: ☐ ROL 1 ☐ ROL 2 ☐ ROL 3 ☐ ROL 4
☐ ROL 5 ☐ ROL 6 ☐ ROL 7 ☐ ROL 8

I am enclosing:

$__________ To purchase cassette series for $44.50 (in Canada $56.50*) which includes the album cover

$__________ To purchase individual cassettes at $5.00 each (in Canada $6.35*)

$__________ Total of purchases

$__________ California residents please add 6 percent sales tax

$__________ *British Columbia residents please add 7 percent sales tax

$__________ Canadian residents please add 6 percent for postage

$__________ U.S. residents please add 10 percent for first-class shipping and handling if desired

$__________ Gift for the Insight for Living radio ministry for which a tax-deductible receipt will be issued

$__________ **TOTAL AMOUNT DUE (please do not send cash)**

Form of payment:

☐ *Check or money order made payable to Insight for Living*

☐ *Credit card (VISA or MasterCard only)*

If there is a balance: ☐ *Apply it as a donation* ☐ *Please refund*

CREDIT CARD PURCHASES:

☐ *VISA* ☐ *MasterCard No.*____________________

*Expiration Date*____________________

*Signature*____________________

We cannot process your credit card purchase without your signature.

*Name*____________________

*Address*____________________

*City*____________________ *Radio Station*__________

*State/Province*________________ *Zip/Postal Code*__________

*Telephone (   )*____________________

Just in case there is a question concerning your order

Mail your order to one of the following addresses:

Insight for Living
Sales Department
Post Office Box 4444
Fullerton, CA 92634

Insight for Living Ministries
Post Office Box 2510
Vancouver, BC
Canada V6B 3W7

If he did take the gospel to Spain, then he was one of the earliest Christians to be a witness " 'both in Jerusalem, and in all Judea and Samaria, and even to the remotest part of the earth' " (Acts 1:8b).

III. Paul's Attitude.

His dream to evangelize the yet unevangelized was both realistic and optimistic. Paul confessed that he had "often been hindered" in his attempts to travel to Rome (v. 22). But he did not allow these hindrances to become permanent roadblocks. For regardless of his circumstances, he continued to look forward to the time when his dream would be realized (v. 29).

IV. Paul's Principles for Us.

There is so much here we can learn from. But among the numerous insights revealed, four are predominant.

- **A. Life's greatest accomplishments are joint efforts.**
- **B. Great accomplishments are seldom achieved without hindrances.**
- **C. Hindrances can be overcome by a sustained focus on the goal.**
- **D. The essential companion of great accomplishments is enthusiasm.**

Living Insights

Study One

As one can quickly observe from the last part of Romans 15, Paul was a real traveler. Perhaps some of the geographical locations he mentioned are unfamiliar to you. If so, then this is a good time to roll out a map and discover where they are.

- Refer to some maps that detail Paul's missionary journeys. You can find them in the back of most Bibles. A Bible atlas would also be a helpful source to use. In order to get a feel for the land during Paul's time, locate the following places:

Cities	**Provinces/Countries**	**Bodies of Water**
Jerusalem	Judea	Mediterranean Sea
Antioch	Samaria	Sea of Galilee
Ephesus	Galilee	Jordan River
Corinth	Galatia	Dead Sea
Philippi	Asia	Nile River
Thessalonica	Greece	Red Sea
Rome	Achaia	
	Macedonia	
	Illyricum	
	Italy	
	Spain	

Living Insights

Study Two

The essential companion of great accomplishments is enthusiasm. Is that statement at home in your life? Take a few minutes to answer the following questions about your personal display of positive living:

- Would people consider you an enthusiastic person? Why or why not?
- Does a person have to be an extrovert in order to be enthusiastic?
- Can you name some things that help you exhibit enthusiasm?
- Can you name some things that hinder you from being enthusiastic?
- How does enthusiasm relate to godliness?

How to Make Prayer Practical

Acts 12:1–16, Romans 15:30–33

For many, the subject of prayer is about as exciting as changing a flat tire. This is probably because the regular practice of prayer is just plain hard work. Indeed, some people find it so boring and difficult that they have become very creative in dodging the responsibility. Yes, for too many Christians prayer has become about as commonly utilized as a fire escape—for emergencies only! This is *not* God's perspective on prayer. In fact, He views it as the most profound and significant discipline of the Christian life. The Apostle Paul reiterates this truth in the latter verses of Romans 15. And in so doing, he relates several guidelines that can help us pray more effectively.

I. How Not to Pray (Acts 12:1–16).

Before we turn to Paul's counsel showing how we should pray, let's zero in on a story in Acts 12 that will reveal how we should not pray.

A. Prayer for Peter's Situation (vv. 1–12). The account opens with Agrippa I on the throne in Judea (v. 1). His political title was Herod. It was used in the same way that the title *senator* or *president* is used in the United States. The text tells us that Agrippa "laid hands on some who belonged to the church, in order to mistreat them." One of the believers he picked up was "James the brother of John" (v. 2a), a prominent leader and apostle in the early Church (cf. Acts 1:13, Gal. 2:9). Agrippa put him to death "with a sword" (Acts 12:2b). When the king saw how pleased the unbelieving Jews were over the execution of James, he arrested the Apostle Peter. Then "he put him in prison, delivering him to four squads of soldiers to guard him, intending after the Passover to bring him out before the people" for public execution (vv. 3–4). This life-threatening situation prompted other Christians to fervently petition God on Peter's behalf (v. 5). The result of their prayers was a first-class miracle:

> And on the very night when Herod was about to bring him forward, Peter was sleeping between two soldiers, bound with two chains; and guards in front of the door were watching over the prison. And behold, an angel of the Lord suddenly appeared, and a light shone in the cell; and he struck Peter's side and roused him, saying, "Get up quickly." And his chains fell off his hands. And the angel said to him, "Gird yourself and put on your sandals." And he did so. And he said to him, "Wrap your cloak around you and follow me." And he went out and continued to follow, and he did not know that what was being done

by the angel was real, but thought he was seeing a vision. And when they had passed the first and second guard, they came to the iron gate that leads into the city, which opened for them by itself; and they went out and went along one street; and immediately the angel departed from him. And when Peter came to himself, he said, "Now I know for sure that the Lord has sent forth His angel and rescued me from the hand of Herod and from all that the Jewish people were expecting." And when he realized this, he went to the house of Mary, the mother of John who was also called Mark, where many were gathered together and were praying. (vv. 6–12)

B. Response to God's Provision (vv. 13–16). We might expect from the incredible miracles God had already performed in the early Church (cf. Acts 2:1–12, 37–41; 3:1–11; 4:23–31; 5:12–25; 9:32–42) that the Christians would be unsurprised to witness another supernatural act. The opposite was, in fact, the case. After being freed from prison, Peter made his way to the house where prayer was being offered, and "he knocked at the door of the gate." In response, "a servant-girl named Rhoda" came to the gate (Acts 12:13). When she recognized Peter's voice, she was so ecstatic that she left the gate locked and returned to the house announcing that Peter was standing outside (v. 14). But none of those who were praying believed her. In spite of her insistence, "they kept saying, 'It is his angel' " (v. 15). These Christians were apparently convinced that their prayers would not be answered. However, they did eventually open the gate as the result of Peter's persistent knocking. The text says that when they saw it was actually Peter, they "were amazed" (v. 16). Rather than believing that God would miraculously answer their fervent request, they doubted Him even when He granted the answer they sought. Although the Lord may fulfill the prayers of doubters, He does not want us to make our requests with an attitude of uncertainty (cf. Matt. 21:21–22, Mark 11:24).

II. How to Pray (Romans 15:30–33).

With this negative example in mind, let's focus in on some positive instruction. In these verses, the Apostle Paul calls on the Christians in Rome to pray with him over an important matter. His words provide four significant guidelines designed to make prayer practical.

A. Make people aware of the need (vv. 30a, 32). We know from the context that Paul had experienced various hindrances which, thus far, had kept him from traveling to Rome. Rather than facing them alone, Paul shared about these barriers with the Roman Christians and urgently asked them to join with him in prayer concerning them (vv. 22, 30a, 32). He did not assume that they knew about his need. Instead, he made them aware of it in order that they might lock arms with him in bringing it before God's throne. Like Paul, we cannot presume that our needs are known to other Christians. We must communicate our requests to them so as to illicit their support in prayer.

B. **Be willing to get involved** (v. 30b). The basis upon which Paul urged the Roman believers to pray was twofold—the "Lord Jesus Christ" and "the love of the Spirit." In other words, he appealed to the divine bond Christians have as members of God's forever family. Since we have the same Lord and are united by the same love, we have all the reason we need to pray for one another. Furthermore, when we do choose to become involved in praying for each other, we commit ourselves to some hard work. This point was underscored by Paul when he called on the Roman Christians to "strive together" with him in their prayers. The Greek word for *strive together* was often employed in athletic contexts. It literally means "to contend along with, to share in a contest." The term conveys the idea of mutual, agonizing perseverance for the attainment of an agreed upon goal. Paul's use of this word in a context of prayer certainly communicates the truth that this spiritual discipline is difficult yet rewarding work. What he says also demonstrates that God designed prayer to be primarily a team effort. In short, the practice of prayer requires a willingness on our part to get involved in the lives of others.

C. **Make your requests specific** (vv. 31–32a). Rather than simply asking his readers to intercede for him, Paul also spelled out the content of his prayer request. His petition contained three elements: (1) deliverance from those who were "disobedient in Judea," (2) approval from the Jerusalem Christians for his service to them in bringing financial relief, and (3) joy in fulfilling his personal goal of finally coming to Rome. The example Paul has set is a good one for us to follow. Like him, we should not be vague in our prayer requests. Rather, we should be as precise as possible so that others can pray more intelligently with us.

D. **Enjoy the rest found in God's will** (vv. 32b–33). When we pray in accord with God's will, we can find refreshing rest and comforting peace. For it is in our willing submission to His perfect plan that we can experience freedom from anxiety. Paul intimated as much when he penned these words to the young pastor Timothy: "First of all, then, I urge that entreaties and prayers, petitions and thanksgivings, be made on behalf of all men ... in order that we may lead a tranquil and quiet life" (1 Tim. 2:1–2).

III. Some Principles on Prayer.

Paul's words concerning the spiritual discipline of prayer remind us again of its importance and practicality. Let's not allow these facts to fade. Instead, let's both persistently apply the guidelines we have discovered and permanently etch into our minds the timeless principles that follow.

A. Prayer is a top priority.

B. Prayer is an urgent essential in life.

C. Prayer is the best tranquilizer on earth.

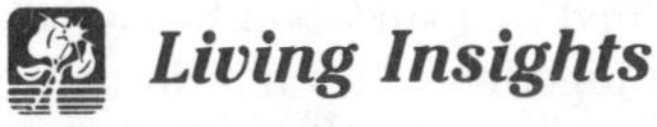

Study One

Do you have any problem making prayer practical? The struggle seems to be a common one among Christians. So let's turn our attention to the Gospels and gain some insight into this matter from the words of Christ.

- Make a copy of the following chart. The two passages listed there hold great truths about prayer. As you read them, translate the concepts they communicate into practical principles on prayer.

Practical Principles on Prayer	
Passages	Principles
Matthew 6:1–15	
John 17:1–26	

Living Insights

Study Two

Based on Romans 15:30–33, the main thrust of this lesson concerns how we should pray. Let's use some of the points we have observed as a series of prayer reminders.

- Below, you can see the four main guidelines on praying effectively. Talk to the Lord about your willingness to be an intercessor, asking Him to provide you with opportunities to follow these directives.
  - —Make people aware of the need.
  - —Be willing to get involved.
  - —Make your requests specific.
  - —Enjoy the rest found in God's will.

You May Kiss the Bride

Romans 16:1–16

Open displays of affection have become increasingly rare in today's Christian circles. In our touch-me-not, keep-your-distance society, we are fast becoming isolated, independent entities fenced on all sides by various shades of formality and cool professionalism. Unfortunately, churches are not immune to this life-threatening disease. We Christians need to take the steps necessary to pierce and permeate our local assemblies with appropriate demonstrations of affection and concern. The Apostle Paul certainly enjoined the Roman believers to do this. And thankfully, the Lord has seen fit to preserve his example for us to follow. So let's lower our guard as Paul unveils how we might show love to one another.

I. A Reminder of Affection (Romans 12–15).
The fondness Paul displays in Romans 16 is not a new manifestation in the letter. We can see several instances of its occurrence in the previous three chapters. Let's briefly review a few of them.

- **A. Romans 12:9–10.** In these verses we are told that genuine love is unhypocritical and displays itself in familial-like devotion.
- **B. Romans 13:10.** Here we learn that authentic love does not wrong another person but, as such, is "the fulfillment of the law."
- **C. Romans 14:15.** This passage suggests that a biblical expression of love will lead to the sacrificing of personal rights for the sake of preserving another believer in the faith.
- **D. Romans 15:30.** In this text we discover that Christian love forms part of the basis and motivation for corporate prayer.

II. A List of Observations (Romans 16:1–16).
As we can see, *agápe* love is person-oriented, service-centered, self-sacrificing, and action-prone. All of these facets of true affection pervade the first half of Romans 16. Let's walk our way through its teaching by (1) gaining a general overview of what the passage says and (2) gleaning a specific understanding of what it means.

- **A. Generally.** A careful perusal of this passage yields at least three major observations. First, *twenty-seven people are mentioned by name.* The fact that Paul remembered all of these individuals in this way implies that he cared about them deeply. Perhaps they were even on his prayer list. Second, *twenty-one titles are associated with these people.* And many of the descriptions given manifest Paul's personal interest in these believers. Here is a sampling: "sister," "servant of the church," "fellow workers in Christ Jesus," "beloved," "kinsmen," and "fellow prisoners" (vv. 1, 3, 5, 7). Third, *nineteen times reference is made to greeting, or commending, a person.* In fact, one of the last references like this gives Christians a general exhortation to "greet one another with a holy kiss" (v. 16a). This kiss was meant to convey spiritual intimacy and affection between believers. When Christians first practiced it, they usually kissed each other on the cheek or forehead. As time went on, however, governmental persecution waned, and with it, this overt expression of Christian love. Now, many believers just shake hands, and even this is usually viewed as a mere formality.

B. Specifically. With these general observations before us, we are ready to discuss the meaning of the text. Among the many truths presented in these sixteen verses, four stand out with crystal clarity.

1. **The Bride of Christ has unified variety.** All Christians comprise the Bride of Christ. But this profound oneness does not disparage their individual differences. For instance, in Romans 16 we find men and women (vv. 1, 11), couples and singles (vv. 3, 13), and spiritually young as well as mature Christians mentioned (vv. 5, 7). We have already learned from other passages that believers are given different gifts, which is another expression of the Church's variety (Rom. 12:6–8). However, all such diversity is to be channeled toward the unification and edification of the Bride, not her division and demise (1 Cor. 12:5–31, Eph. 4:11–16).
2. **The Bride of Christ has obscure servants.** There are many Christians who diligently minister without ever receiving a spot in the limelight. Several examples are provided in the final chapter of Romans. Here Paul mentions some people whom we would never know existed, much less what they did, if he had failed to name them. One of these background workers was Phoebe. Paul describes her as a *servant*—that is, "deaconess"—of the Cenchrean church (v. 1).* Most Bible students agree that she was the one who delivered the Epistle of Romans to its original readers. That is why Paul commends her to the Roman Christians and asks them to "receive her in the Lord in a manner worthy of the saints" (vv. 1a, 2a). This is the only place in Scripture where Phoebe is mentioned. Yet what a significant role she played when she delivered the Magna Charta of Christianity to Rome!

*For additional information on deaconesses in the early Church, see the study guide titled *Excellence in Ministry* (Fullerton: Insight for Living), pp. 55–56.

3. **The Bride of Christ has humble esteem.** Among the individuals Paul names are some whose honor and courage were renown. However, it is never suggested that they were flaunting the great respect they had received. Two of these persons were Prisca (also called Priscilla) and Aquila, a husband and wife team (v. 3). Paul first met them when he arrived in Corinth on his second missionary journey (Acts 18:1–2). While in that city, Paul lived and worked with this couple (Acts 18:3). After about eighteen months had passed, Paul left Corinth and went to Ephesus, taking with him Prisca and Aquila (vv. 18–19). He left them behind when he departed from Ephesus (v. 19). Some time later, a man named Apollos came to Ephesus and was greatly ministered to by this married team (vv. 24–26). As a result, Apollos left for Corinth and was better able to effectively serve the believers there (Acts 18:27–19:1a, 1 Cor. 3:5–6). It is this faithful couple whom Paul fondly calls "fellow workers in Christ Jesus" and identifies as those who "risked their own necks" to save his life (Rom. 16:3–4a). And yet, nowhere do we read of Prisca and Aquila pridefully declaring their achievements to others. Indeed, they seem to be perfect illustrations of Proverbs 27:2, which states, "Let another praise you, and not your own mouth; a stranger, and not your own lips."
4. **The Bride of Christ has simplified love.** Paul expresses his deep affection for these individuals in the simplest manner. He waves no banners, offers no bouquets, and hands out no trophies. Instead, he honors them in very straightforward, unsplashy terms. Notice some of the words he uses: "I commend," "greet," "I give thanks," "has worked hard," "approved in Christ," "workers in the Lord," and "a choice man in the Lord" (vv. 1, 3, 4, 6, 10, 12, 13). This shows us that Christian love does not have to be expressed in a grandiose manner. Indeed, it is often best manifested in unimpressive yet authentic ways.

III. A Series of Suggestions.

So how may we kiss the Bride in an affectionate and appropriate manner? What can we do to express our love to other Christians? The answers lie in the personal application of these four suggestions.

A. Accept the variety in others.
B. Become a servant of others.
C. Cultivate expressions of esteem for others.
D. Declare your love to others.

Living Insights

Study One

Twenty-seven persons are mentioned by name in Romans 16:1–16. How many of these are familiar to you?

- On a copy of the following chart record all the names in Romans 16:1–16. Using a concordance and the marginal notes in your Bible, look up any other references listed on these individuals. This should help you create some mini-biographies of these people.

Mini-biographies—Romans 16:1–16		
Names	References	Notes

Living Insights

Study Two

This is the sort of passage that we tend to move through quickly. Instead of doing this, let's use these verses as a basis for discussion. Gather together some family or friends and use the following ideas to guide you through the material.

- Read Romans 12:9–10, 13:10, 14:15, and 15:30. Determine what one thing each passage has in common. Then discuss which reference means the most to you and why. Try to be specific as you share your thoughts. Then thoughtfully read 1 Corinthians 13:1–7.
- Read the first two verses of Romans 16. Discuss what it means to be a servant (v. 1) and a helper (v. 2). Why are these two roles so difficult to carry out? Talk about the benefits that occur when we help and serve others with a good attitude. Share with the group some creative ways to go about being a servant; then develop a practical plan and implement it.
- Paul mentions *Prisca* and *Aquila* by name in Romans 16:3. Do a little research on this couple by reading Acts 18:1–2, 18–26. What are some characteristics that stand out to you? In Romans 16:4, Paul says that they "risked their own necks" for him. For whom would you risk your life? Thank God for that person.
- Romans 16:7 mentions a person who was "outstanding among the apostles." And verse 13 talks about "a choice man in the Lord." How are these characteristics cultivated? Describe three things you feel are essential in becoming a person of this caliber. Are there any Scriptures that come to your mind which support your answers?
- Romans 16:16a encourages the brothers and sisters in God's family to "greet one another with a holy kiss" (cf. 1 Cor. 16:20, 2 Cor. 13:12, 1 Thess. 5:26). Why don't we see that in the Body today? Talk about how we can show affection in our local assemblies.

When Trouble Is Brewing

Romans 16:17–20

The early Church, so often idealized, certainly had its problems. Contention and dissension were not uncommon among the local Christian assemblies. Sometimes these difficulties were caused by infighting among believers. On other occasions serious disputes arose because false teachers gained a foothold in a church and used their position to initiate and perpetuate divisions. Whatever the means, the results were often the same: some Christians fell prey to false doctrine and immoral behavior. What happened then still occurs today. However, the tide can be turned if we will consistently apply the counsel Paul gives in Romans 16:17–20. Through these verses the Lord has provided us with timeless wisdom. Now it is up to us to work it out in life.

I. In the past, trouble has occurred.

We can develop a better understanding of various topics discussed in Scripture by gaining a historical perspective on them. So let's do that now with regard to church dissensions.

A. In the Early Church. The New Testament is replete with references to local assemblies that were experiencing internal strife. For example, in the church at Antioch, debate arose over the issue of the relationship between circumcision and salvation (Acts 14:26–15:2). The dissension created over this question was so heated that an official church council was called in Jerusalem to settle the issue (Acts 15:2–35). The Epistle of Galatians was written to address a similar problem that had developed among the believers in the region of Galatia. At least two letters were sent to the Corinthian church attempting to resolve disputes over such matters as favoritism, the extent of Christian liberty, sexual immorality, divorce and remarriage, spiritual gifts, and the bodily Resurrection of Christ. Paul exhorted two Christian women in the church at Philippi not to fight with one another but "to live in harmony in the Lord" (Phil. 4:2). And the Apostle John spent a few verses in one of his letters addressing some problems caused by a self-appointed, bossy church leader named Diotrephes. Observe what he said:

> I wrote something to the church; but Diotrephes, who loves to be first among them, does not accept what we say. For this reason, if I come, I will call attention to his deeds which he does, unjustly accusing us with wicked words; and not satisfied with this, neither does he himself receive the brethren, and he forbids those who desire to do so, and puts them out of the church. (3 John 9–10)

B. In These Last Days. Since the first century, ecclesiastical friction has not passed away. Churches today still experience dissension over a number of issues. Besides the all-too-common moral and relational problems that promote divisions, there are a number of theological issues that cause waves of disturbance. Some of these are the inerrancy of Scripture, the role of women in the Church, the permissibility of divorce and remarriage, the relationship between Christians and governing authorities, the ordination of homosexuals, the charismatic movement, the social responsibility of believers, the roles of husbands and wives, and the justifiability of abortion. All of these issues are important, and they all need to be resolved on biblical grounds. However, the controversies that rage over them have generally created more heat and disunity than light and harmony.

II. In Rome, trouble was occurring.

As we step back into the first century, we discover that the Roman church was not an exception to the norm. She too was beginning to experience the birth pangs of strife. Because Paul was aware of this, he issued a strong warning to her members and coupled it with some timeless counsel. Let's carefully examine what he said in Romans 16:17–20.

A. What was happening? Paul answers this question for us in verse 17. First, there were individuals in the Roman assembly who were causing "dissensions." This term in the original Greek language does not refer to disagreements, but it does denote divisiveness and polarization. The only other New Testament reference to this word is in Galatians 5:19–20. Here "dissensions" is listed among "the deeds of the flesh." And in that context, Paul forewarns his readers that "those who practice such things shall not inherit the kingdom of God" (v. 21). Second, those who were causing dissensions in the Roman church were also creating "hindrances" (Rom. 16:17a). They were setting and baiting traps of offense for the believers there. Third, these agents of disunity were promoting doctrines and morals that ran "contrary to the teaching" of orthodox Christianity (v. 17b). In other words, these were instructors of heresy who knowingly sought to subvert the truth of God.

B. Why was it happening? Verse 18 tells us: "For such men are slaves, not of our Lord Christ but of their own appetites; and by their smooth and flattering speech they deceive the hearts of the unsuspecting." The heretics in the Roman church were apparently passing themselves off as Christians, when in reality they were enslaved to pleasing themselves. In another letter, the Apostle Paul referred to people like this as "enemies of the cross of Christ, whose end is destruction, whose god is their appetite, and whose glory is in their shame" (Phil. 3:18b–19a). Returning to the situation in Romans, we are told that the false teachers were smooth-talking the gullible and naive away from the Christian faith. Stated another way, undiscerning believers were being led astray by unbelieving deceivers.

C. **How was it to be handled?** Paul exhorted the Roman Christians to counteract the divisive individuals in their midst through two means. The first one was *scrutinizing observation* (Rom. 16:17a). He told the believers to keep a close eye on what these people taught and how they behaved. The second action these Christians were to take was *discerning separation* (v. 17b). The Roman believers—most likely, the church leaders—were to take the steps necessary to block any inroads that had been or could be made into the congregation by the false teachers.

A Clarifying Comment

We would be amiss if we understood Paul's instruction here to mean that Christians should have no contact with non-Christians. This interpretation is flatly contradicted by the example of Jesus and the teaching of Scripture. Christ spent a good deal of His earthly ministry with unbelievers of diverse backgrounds and religious persuasions. Indeed, He associated with them so much that He gained the reputation of being " 'a gluttonous man and a drunkard, a friend of tax-gatherers and sinners' " (Matt. 11:19b; cf. Luke 5:29–32). In the Bible, we are encouraged to develop relationships with non-Christians (for example, see Matt. 28:19; John 20:21–23; Acts 1:8, 8:26–40, 9:1–22). One of the clearest passages in this regard is 1 Corinthians 5. There the Apostle Paul clears up a misconception concerning something he had written to the believers in Corinth. Pay close attention to what he says: "I wrote you in my letter not to associate with immoral people; I did not at all mean with the immoral people of this world, or with the covetous and swindlers, or with idolaters; for then you would have to go out of the world. But actually, I wrote to you not to associate with any so-called brother if he should be an immoral person, or covetous, or an idolater, or a reviler, or a drunkard, or a swindler—not even to eat with such a one" (1 Cor. 5:9–11). In other words, Christians cannot and should not avoid contact with non-Christians; but rather, they should disassociate themselves from Christians who persist in living like non-Christians. Given all of this, we may understand Paul's instruction in Romans 16:17 to be as follows: First, *Christians should avoid unbelievers who are genuine threats to the maintenance of their Christian faith.* And second, *churches should take adequate measures to protect their members from those unbelievers who would attempt to lure the less discerning believers away from the Christian truth.*

D. How could it be overcome? Paul was not a pessimist. He knew that the Christians in Rome could restore their unity. The solution rested in their enactment of three guidelines. First, they would need to *continue in obedience* (v. 19a). As long as they conscientiously sought to apply Christianity, they would be able to undercut the subversive activities of those heretics in their midst. Second, they were to *apply moral wisdom* (v. 19b). They needed to grow in their practice of good—another activity that would increase their unity and decrease their susceptibility to becoming divided. Third, Paul exhorted them to *separate from evil* (v. 19c). He did not want the Roman believers to even entertain the idea of adopting the heretics' doctrine and lifestyle. Instead, they were to immerse themselves in truth and goodness, not error and evil.

III. In our churches, trouble can occur.

What happened in the first-century Roman church can occur in any of our twentieth-century congregations. How can we protect ourselves against such situations? Paul suggests a two-pronged defense.

A. Remain alert to the obvious clues. We can know that trouble is brewing when we observe any of these three signs: (1) dissension in the church, (2) disobedience to the Scriptures, and (3) deception from the heart.

B. Start taking the best medicines. Here are three preventive prescriptions: (1) gain a working knowledge of the Bible, (2) maintain a watchful eye over the flock of God, and (3) grow in our willpower to reject error.

Living Insights

Study One

"When Trouble Is Brewing" is not only an appropriate title for this portion of Romans, but it also typifies three letters in the New Testament. Let's take a closer look at these epistles of John.

- Copy the following chart into your notebook. As you read through 1, 2, and 3 John, look for two types of phrasing—*descriptions* of trouble brewing and *solutions* for the simmering problems.

When Trouble Is Brewing—1, 2, and 3 John			
Troubles Described	Verses	Troubles Solved	Verses

Living Insights

Study Two

Our study has shown that trouble was occurring in the Roman church. Problems may be present in your local assembly as well. Are you looking for the obvious clues and preparing yourself with the best medicines?

- Look over the following points reiterated from this lesson. Write down your observations of potential troubles brewing in your church. Also note some actions you might take to prevent these from ever beginning to take hold and grow.

Obvious Clues

—Dissension in the Church
—Disobedience to the Scriptures
—Deception from the Heart

Best Medicines

—Working Knowledge of the Bible
—Watchful Eye over the Flock of God
—Willpower to Reject Error

Unseen Evil and Uplifting Good

Romans 16:17–24

The Bible is a book of sharp contrasts—light and dark, obedience and disobedience, belief and unbelief, joy and sorrow, victory and defeat, honesty and deceit, God and Satan, heaven and hell. Such black-and-white differences help us to discover what our standard should be for daily living. They expose the extremes and beckon us to choose between them. The middle verses of Romans 16 provide an example of yet another contrast—unseen and insidious evil as opposed to visible and encouraging good. As usual, the contrast reveals some significant insights about how we should live.

I. Awareness of the Evil (Romans 16:17–20a).

In the last lesson we found Paul issuing a strong warning to the Roman Christians. He urged them to watch out for unbelievers who were parading as believers. These individuals were intent on deceiving "the hearts of the unsuspecting" (vv. 17–18). The Apostle then went on to lay down three guidelines that would help the Roman saints deal with the false teachers in their midst. They were (1) the faithful continuance in obedience to God's Word, (2) the consistent application of moral wisdom, and (3) the determined separation from evil (v. 19). Paul drew his warning and remedy to a close with this intriguing statement of victory: "And the God of peace will soon crush Satan under your feet" (v. 20a). Before we can gain understanding and comfort from this passage, we need to come to grips with some key terms and important background material.

A. Some Key Terms Explained. The Greek word for *crush* in verse 20 means "to shatter or break into pieces." This term conveys the idea of being completely nullified and ruined. The other major word in this text is the Greek term for *soon,* which literally means "quickly." When we apply these meanings to the passage, we can translate it to read like this: "And the God of peace will quickly ruin Satan under your feet." But when and on what conditions will God accomplish this? We need to review some essential background data in order to answer this query.

B. Some Crucial Background Reviewed. The first mention in Scripture of Satan's defeat is found in the Book of Genesis. Its opening chapters introduce us to the beautiful Creation, full of innocence and void of evil (Gen. 1–2). However, once we dip into chapter 3, the scene begins to change. A crafty serpent is seen conversing with Eve. He convinces her to disobey God by partaking of the fruit from the forbidden tree. She then tempts Adam to eat of the tree. At that moment in history, innocence was defiled and evil gained a victory. But such a situation was not destined to last. God passed judgment on the serpent's sin in these words:

> "And I will put enmity
> Between you and the woman,
> And between your seed and her seed;
> He shall bruise you on the head,
> And you shall bruise him on the heel." (Gen. 3:15)

In this prophecy, *her seed* refers to the Messiah who would eventually come from the line of Adam and Eve (cf. Luke 3:23, 38). The Hebrew word translated *bruise* means "to crush." It carries the idea of utter defeat. So the Lord told the serpent, who was Satan, that he would defeat the Messiah, but only on the heel. This suggests that Satan's victory would be temporary. On the other hand, God said that the Messiah would crush Satan on the head, which speaks of a permanent victory. Satan's battle was won when Jesus was crucified at Calvary. When the prophet Isaiah looked forward to that day, he said of the Messiah,

> He was pierced through for our transgressions,
> He was crushed for our iniquities. (Isa. 53:5a)

Jesus' death marked a victory for evil, for the very exemplification of goodness was maliciously and wrongfully executed. However, when Christ rose bodily from the dead, He ascended to His rightful place of honor and authority with the Heavenly Father. Through these actions, He wielded the deathblow to both Satan and sin (Col. 2:15). Although the war between Good and evil has been won, battles are still being waged by the enemies of Good (Eph. 6:10–16). Satan and his cohorts are committed to engaging the Lord and His people in warfare. However, these demons eventually will be cast into the pit of hell to suffer unending judgment (Rev. 20:10–15).

C. **The Central Meaning Exposed.** After considering this material, we are now prepared to grasp the interpretation of Romans 16:20a. Paul tells the Roman believers that being "wise in what is good, and innocent in what is evil" (v. 19b) results in the swift defeat of Satan by God. The devil will not experience even brief victories over Christians who refuse to fall prey to his enticements and who apply God's counsel in Scripture. This is true for all believers. We do not have to be intimidated by a foe who has already lost the war. If we stand firm in obedience to God, we will find His resources sufficient to trod down our archenemy Satan.

II. Encouragement from the Good (Romans 16:20b–24). Following Paul's warning, we discover a section dedicated to uplifting the believer. In this passage, he naturally turns from the peace of God to the grace of Christ. The result is a passage that suggests three major realms of encouragement: Christ, others, and ourselves. Let's briefly examine each one.

A. Grace from Christ (vv. 20b, 24). Both of these verses are practically identical, and they emphasize the same theme—the grace of Jesus Christ. It's appropriate that this major thought of Romans is reiterated here. As we may recall, divine grace signifies the unmerited, unrepayable favor God grants to sinners. When we reach out and accept by faith His gift of grace, we are freed forever from everlasting death. From that wonderful moment of conversion onward, we stand justified before the holy King of all. And since it is His grace that saves us, it is His grace that should govern our lives. The appropriation of undeserved favor should permeate our beings so much that we mirror Christ's character in all we think, say, and do. As this occurs, we will find ourselves emancipated from the self-imposed guilt and exhaustion that results from trying to earn God's favor.

B. Support from Others (vv. 21–23). In these verses Paul mentions eight fellow Christians who had been encouraging him. Apparently, they had wanted to send their greetings to the believers in Rome. The first person on Paul's list is Timothy (v. 21a). He was converted under Paul's ministry and chosen to assist him in his many tasks (Acts 16:1–3). We have two letters that Paul sent to him—1 and 2 Timothy. The next individual Paul mentions is Lucius (Rom. 16:21b). This may be a reference to Luke, the physician and writer of the Gospel of Luke as well as the Book of Acts. However, if Lucius is to be considered along with Jason and Sosipater as Paul's "kinsmen"—that is, his relatives—then Lucius cannot be identified as Luke. For that would make Lucius a Jewish Christian, whereas Luke was a Gentile believer (cf. Col. 4:10–11, 14). At any rate, these men supported Paul in his ministry, and at least two of them were blood relatives. The fifth person introduced himself as Tertius (Rom. 16:22). He acted as Paul's secretary in the composition of Romans. Next, Gaius is named as the one who had extended his hospitality to both Paul and the young Corinthian church (v. 23a). Gaius may have been the same individual as Titius Justus, who is mentioned in Acts 18:7 in association with the establishment of the church in Corinth. The treasurer of Corinth, Erastus, also sent his greetings to the Roman Christians

(Rom. 16:23b).* The last individual Paul lists is "Quartus, the brother" (v. 23c). His name is Latin for "fourth," while Tertius' name also stands as the Latin designation for "third." This may mean that Quartus and Tertius were brothers, their names indicating the order in which they were born into their family. The similarity may also suggest that they were slaves, for in the Roman system, slaves were given numbers for identification. If this was the case, then it is likely that they were being loaned out to Paul by their owner. So Paul was not only encouraged by city officials; he was also supported by common slaves. This demonstrates that where grace abounds, classifications diminish in significance. All Christians are important to God regardless of their status in life.

C. **Confidence from Ourselves** (v. 24). In this verse we read, "The grace of our Lord Jesus Christ be with you all. Amen." Paul is confident that Christ's grace will sustain the believers in Rome. So he declares that fact with authority in order to encourage them. In essence he is saying, "I believe that Christ's grace will accompany you; now you believe it too. Let grace characterize your life."

III. Application for Today.

There are many insights we may glean from these verses in Romans. Among them, three stand out from the rest.

A. **We dare not ignore the presence of evil.** If certain people or circumstances are not trying to pull us down, then Satan is. Spiritual warfare is real. We can try to ignore it, but only to our own peril.

B. **We need not be intimidated by evil.** Because Satan has lost the war, we do not have to tremble under his attacks. As long as we are clothed in the armor of God, we can withstand any charge he mounts against us (Eph. 6:10–17).

C. **We will not experience victory until we appropriate grace on a personal level.** God thwarts Satan; we do not. If we try to fight the devil on our own, we will become terribly bruised. However, if we confront him by consistently walking in the wisdom of grace, then God will quickly crush him under our feet.

*Archaeological excavations have identified this Erastus with a civic official of the same name who paid for a stretch of pavement in first-century Corinth (see F. F. Bruce, *The Epistle of Paul to the Romans,* Tyndale New Testament Commentaries, Grand Rapids: William B. Eerdmans Publishing Co., 1963, p. 280).

Living Insights

Study One

Perhaps by now you find yourself saying, "There's much more to this last chapter of Romans than I expected." If so, you're absolutely right!

- Let's return to a previously used Bible study method—*paraphrasing*. Take the first twenty-four verses of Romans 16 and write them out in your own words. Remember, this is to help you get into the meanings of the words and the feelings that rest at the heart of this passage. You'll be amazed at how a list of names can really come to life!

Living Insights

Study Two

Grace . . . an unfathomable concept. Yet we are admonished in this study to appropriate it on a personal level. What does that really involve anyway? Perhaps the following questions will help lead your thinking in the right direction.

- What is entailed in appropriating grace in your relationship with God?
- What is involved in appropriating grace in your relationships with others?
- What is required in appropriating grace in your understanding of yourself?
- How does guilt "do a number" on grace?
- How do our obligations to God affect grace?
- How should we understand the relationship between grace and human merit?

To God Be the Glory Forever

Romans 16:25–27

Woven into the tapestry of Romans are three doxologies. The first one occurs in the final verse of chapter 11. The next one appears in chapter 15, verse 33. The last and longest one is appropriately found at the end of the letter. Each of these benedictions raises our eyes to God by emphasizing one or more of His numerous attributes. The final doxology in this epistle unveils some of the most significant truths about God present anywhere in the Bible. The result is a passage of praise that highly exalts the plan, wisdom, and glory of the Blessed King.

I. To God . . .

It is fitting that the Magna Charta of the Christian faith end with a glorious tribute to its divine Author. Paul, the inspired human writer, breaks forth with words of encouragement and assurance that point to God as their source, support, and goal. The largest portion of this benediction focuses on four truths concerning the almighty Lord and His plan for man.

A. The Giver of Stability (v. 25a). The verse opens with these words, "Now to Him who is able to establish you . . ." The Greek term translated *to establish* means "to prop up, make firm, make stable." It conveys the idea of something holding up or supporting something else. In this context, the thought is that God is the One who has the power to stabilize us. Much earlier in the letter, Paul said that he longed to see the Roman Christians in order to establish them (Rom. 1:11). However, given what he says in this final benediction, it appears he has learned through writing this epistle that the Source of a believer's support is God. Other believers can, at best, be instruments of His stabilizing power. They may help us stand strong during difficult times. But only God is the very foundation of all strength, and only He will never fail to sustain us.

B. The Revealer of the Gospel (vv. 25a–26a). Here Paul informs us that God establishes Christians "according to my gospel and the preaching of Jesus Christ" (v. 25a). The Greek equivalent of the English word *and* is *kaí.* In some instances, such as this one, it is better rendered "that is." Thus, Paul is saying that the content of the gospel is the teaching of Christ. And since Jesus taught that He is the focal point and summation of God's revelation to man (Luke 24:27; John 5:39, 46–47), then He must be the central revelation of the Triune God (cf. John 1:18, Heb. 1:1–3a). In other words, the Father has always unveiled Himself to man through His Son in the power of the Spirit. Therefore, the only way anyone can come to God is through

Jesus Christ. There is no other path that leads to Him. In addition to this, Paul says that the Lord establishes believers "according to the revelation of the mystery which has been kept secret for long ages past, but now is manifested, and by the Scriptures of the prophets, according to the commandment of the eternal God" (vv. 25b–26a). The Greek term for *mystery* is similar in meaning to the English word *secret.* It denotes the idea of something previously hidden and unknown that is now being revealed and understood. The mystery Paul refers to here is clearly spelled out in his letter to the Ephesians. In this book we discover that what God kept secret from man until the first century was the indiscriminate uniting of Jews and Gentiles into one spiritual community. This unification was to be done through the same means—personal faith in Jesus Christ as Savior (Eph. 2:11–3:12). The founding of the universal Church was always a part of God's plan, but it took many centuries before He finally brought it to fruition in history and revealed it to man's inquiring mind.

C. The Proclaimer to the Nations (v. 26b). The gracious Lord has initiated His plan of salvation, not for just a select few, but for the entire world (John 3:16). Therefore, He has made it "known to all the nations" (Rom. 16:26b). This does not mean that everyone has already heard the good news about Christ, but it does show us that the revelation of the gospel is available to all peoples without partiality. Since the Savior's focus is on the world, ours should be also. His mandate is that we proclaim the message of salvation by faith through Christ alone to everyone (Matt. 28:19–20). Some will believe, and others will not. Our job is not to pick and choose to whom we will share. Rather, God calls on us to faithfully declare the good news and consistently apply it wherever we are.

D. The Initiator of Obedience (v. 26c). Paul ends this section of the doxology by noting that it is the Lord who leads individuals to the "obedience of faith." Our task is not to convert anyone. Only God causes people to be born again (1 Pet. 1:3). After all, if we cannot save ourselves, how much less able are we to save anyone else! On the other hand, Scripture clearly states that the Lord has chosen human beings to act as His witnesses in the salvation process (Rom. 10:13–15). He has given us the responsibility of getting the message out, while He has graciously accepted the role that no one else could ever fill—Redeemer.

II. . . . Be the Glory Forever.

Since God is unlimited in His nature, no finite creature can fully comprehend Him. Thus, we cannot form a mental or material image that portrays His inexhaustible being. When we try to construct a picture of Him, all we end up with is a dead idol, not the living Lord. This truth is clearly manifested in the first part of Romans 16:27, which reads, "To the only wise God, through Jesus Christ, be the glory forever." There we learn four key facts about God.

A. His Uniqueness. The word *only* expresses the truth that the all-powerful King of the Bible is God alone. He makes this point quite clear through the prophet Isaiah:

> "I am the Lord, and there is no other;
> Besides Me there is no God.
> I will gird you, though you have not known Me;
> That men may know from the rising to the setting
> of the sun
> That there is no one besides Me.
> I am the Lord, and there is no other." (Isa. 45:5–6)

The affirmation that there is just one God is also a declaration of His uniqueness. There is no other being like Him. He is one of a kind, incomparable, unrivaled, matchless, and unsurpassed. We cannot reduce Him to anything in creation, for He far exceeds anything we know now or ever could know.

B. His Wisdom. The one God is also infinitely "wise." This means not only that He is supremely intelligent and knows all things, but also that He is unfathomably perceptive and accurate in His purposes and plans. No wonder Paul could exclaim:

> Oh, the depth of the riches both of the wisdom and knowledge of God! How unsearchable are His judgments and unfathomable His ways! For who has known the mind of the Lord, or who became His counselor? (Rom. 11:33–34)

C. His Son. The primary, revelatory link between the infinite God and finite man is God the Son, Jesus Christ. Without Him, there would be no visible manifestation of God that we could even partially comprehend (John 1:14, 18; 6:46; cf. 1 Tim. 6:16). Similarly, there would be no way for us to come before God free from condemnation without the redemptive work of His Son. Perhaps that is why Paul gives his benediction "through Jesus Christ" (Rom. 16:27a).

D. His Eternal Glory. The doxology closes by ascribing glory to the eternal God forever (v. 27b). His glory is the visible manifestation of His character. The fullest revelation of the Lord's glory is Jesus Christ. As the Gospel of John states, "The Word became flesh, and dwelt among us, and we beheld His glory, glory as of the only begotten from the Father, full of grace and truth" (John 1:14). Furthermore, the glory of God is eternal, not just everlasting. Theologically speaking, the term *everlasting* describes something that has a beginning but no end, while the word *eternal* denotes something that has neither a beginning nor an end. The Lord of the universe is eternal, not everlasting. Therefore, His glory is beginningless and endless, not simply endless.

III. Amen.

The last word in the Book of Romans is simply "Amen." It does not convey the idea of "I hope, wish, or think this is true." Rather, it expresses the deep conviction that "I believe it is true!" Do *you* believe what we have studied? If not, then you are still lost in your sin. You need to embrace the truths in this letter and place your trust in Jesus Christ. However, if you have experienced the Lord's salvation and now stand free from the penalty of sin, then begin to apply the teaching of this book to your life. The sovereign God has promised that He will empower you to live in a manner which is pleasing to Him. But He will not force you into submission. So you must begin obeying His Word. And as you do, He will conform you into the image of His perfect Son. What better life or goal could we ever wish for?

Living Insights

Study One

This study has taught us not only the academics but also the practicalities of relating to others in love. As has been our custom, we will use the final "Living Insights" to *review* where we've been in our study.

- After you've copied the following chart, flip through your Bible, study guide, and notebook in order to refresh your memory about the truths you've gained in this study. Then identify one statement that represents the most important truth you've learned in each lesson.

Relating to Others in Love	
Titles	**Statements of Truth**
How Faith Functions	
Love Exposed	
You and Your Enemy	
How to Be a Godly Rebel	
Legal Tender and Loving Care	
Wake Up and Get Dressed!	
Taboo or Not Taboo?	
Liberty on a Tightrope	
We Are One . . . or Are We?	
Competent Christians	
Preaching and Truckin'	
How to Make Prayer Practical	
You May Kiss the Bride	
When Trouble Is Brewing	
Unseen Evil and Uplifting Good	
To God Be the Glory Forever	

Living Insights

Study Two

When we evaluate the benefits of Bible study, one stands out far above the rest—its ability to affect our lives. Yes, if we let it, the wise application of Bible knowledge can be life-changing!

- Although this chart looks identical to the one previously presented, there is one important difference. This time, as you conduct a review, look for those applications of the text that have changed the way you live. Try to identify one "life-changer" from each of the lessons in this series.

Relating to Others in Love	
Titles	Life-Changers
How Faith Functions	
Love Exposed	
You and Your Enemy	
How to Be a Godly Rebel	
Legal Tender and Loving Care	
Wake Up and Get Dressed!	
Taboo or Not Taboo?	
Liberty on a Tightrope	
We Are One . . . or Are We?	
Competent Christians	
Preaching and Truckin'	
How to Make Prayer Practical	
You May Kiss the Bride	
When Trouble Is Brewing	
Unseen Evil and Uplifting Good	
To God Be the Glory Forever	

Books for Probing Further

Relationships—life would be empty without them. And yet, fewer things are more difficult to begin, develop, and maintain than these. The Lord certainly realized this fact when He moved the Apostle Paul to pen Romans 12–16. There we have learned about God's principles and methods for relating to others in love. Now we know that our relationships with both believers and unbelievers can best flower when our bond to divine Love is strengthened. However, we have also seen that our spiritual growth in Christ is often prompted when we let down our guard and reach out to other human beings. In other words, there is a reciprocal relationship between our dedication to God and our service to people. Our development in each realm is dependent on our progression in the other. This being so, we have chosen to list various resources that will provide additional insight and challenge for your walk with God and your journey with others through life. These sources will act as helpful supplements to your study in the Scriptures.

I. Relating to the Revealer of Love.

Baughen, Michael. *Breaking the Prayer Barrier: Getting through to God.* Foreword by James I. Packer. Wheaton: Harold Shaw Publishers, 1981.

Benson, Bob. *He Speaks Softly: Learning to Hear God's Voice.* Waco: Word Books, 1985.

Bounds, E. M. *Power through Prayer.* Springdale: Whitaker House, 1982.

Bunyan, John. *The Annotated Pilgrim's Progress.* Edited by Warren W. Wiersbe. Chicago: Moody Press, 1980.

Dunn, Charles W. *The Upstream Christian in a Downstream World.* Wheaton: Victor Books, 1979.

Ferguson, Sinclair B. *Grow in Grace.* Colorado Springs: NavPress, 1981.

Friesen, Garry. *Decision Making and the Will of God: A Biblical Alternative to the Traditional View.* With J. Robin Maxson. A Critical Concern Book. Portland: Multnomah Press, 1980.

Hinten, Marvin. *God Is Not a Vending Machine . . . so Why Do We Pray Like He Is?* Grand Rapids: Zondervan Publishing House, 1983.

Hocking, David L. *Pleasing God.* Foreword by Tim LaHaye. San Bernardino: Here's Life Publishers, Inc., 1984.

Knowles, Andrew. *Discovering Prayer.* A Lion Manual. Belleville: Lion Publishing Corporation, 1985. This book has been designed specifically for teenagers.

Laney, J. Carl. *Marching Orders.* Wheaton: Victor Books, 1983.

MacDonald, Gordon. *Ordering Your Private World.* Chicago: Moody Press, 1984.

Machen, J. Gresham. *God Transcendent.* Edited by Ned Bernard Stonehouse. Carlisle: The Banner of Truth Trust, 1982.

Mitchell, Curtis C. *Praying Jesus' Way: A New Approach to Personal Prayer.* Foreword by Joyce Landorf. Old Tappan: Fleming H. Revell Co., 1977.

Murray, Andrew. *The Blessings of Obedience.* Springdale: Whitaker House, 1984.

Peace, Richard. *Pilgrimage: A Handbook on Christian Growth.* Foreword by Lyman Coleman. Grand Rapids: Baker Book House, 1976.

Peterson, Eugene H. *Earth and Altar: The Community of Prayer in a Self-bound Society.* Downers Grove: InterVarsity Press, 1985.
Peterson, Eugene H. *A Long Obedience in the Same Direction.* Downers Grove: InterVarsity Press, 1980.
Schaeffer, Francis A. *True Spirituality.* Wheaton: Tyndale House Publishers, 1971.
Sproul, R. C. *Effective Prayer.* Wheaton: Tyndale House Publishers, Inc., 1984.
Sproul, R. C. *God's Will and the Christian.* Wheaton: Tyndale House Publishers, Inc., 1984.
Swindoll, Charles R. *God's Will: Biblical Direction for Living.* Portland: Multnomah Press, 1981.
Swindoll, Charles R. *Prayer.* Waco: Word Books, 1984.
White, Jerry. *The Power of Commitment.* The Christian Character Library. Colorado Springs: NavPress, 1985.
White, John. *The Fight: A Practical Handbook for Christian Living.* Downers Grove: InterVarsity Press, 1976.
Willard, Dallas. *In Search of Guidance: Developing a Conversational Relationship with God.* Ventura: Regal Books, 1984.
Yohn, Rick. *Beyond Spiritual Gifts.* Wheaton: Tyndale House Publishers, Inc., 1976.

II. Relating to the Receivers of Love.

Baker, Don. *Beyond Forgiveness: The Healing Touch of Church Discipline.* Portland: Multnomah Press, 1984.
Crabb, Lawrence J., Jr., and Allender, Dan B. *Encouragement: The Key to Caring.* Grand Rapids: Zondervan Publishing House, 1984.
Dobson, Edward. *In Search of Unity: An Appeal to Fundamentalists and Evangelicals.* Nashville: Thomas Nelson Publishers, 1985.
Eims, LeRoy. *Disciples in Action.* Colorado Springs: NavPress; Wheaton: Victor Books, 1981.
Getz, Gene A. *Serving One Another.* Wheaton: Victor Books, 1984.
Getz, Gene A. *Sharpening the Focus of the Church.* Foreword by George W. Peters. Chicago: Moody Press, 1974.
Hembree, Ron. *The Speck in Your Brother's Eye.* Old Tappan: Fleming H. Revell Co., 1985.
Hilt, James. *How to Have a Better Relationship with Anybody.* Chicago: Moody Press, 1984.
Howard, J. Grant. *The Trauma of Transparency: A Biblical Approach to Inter-personal Communication.* A Critical Concern Book. Portland: Multnomah Press, 1979.
Hull, Bill. *Jesus Christ Disciplemaker.* Foreword by Joe Aldrich. Colorado Springs: NavPress, 1984.
Inrig, Gary. *Quality Friendship.* Foreword by Erwin W. Lutzer. Chicago: Moody Press, 1981.
Kruse, Colin G. *New Testament Models for Ministry: Jesus and Paul.* Nashville: Thomas Nelson Publishers, 1983.
Little, Paul. *How to Give Away Your Life.* Foreword by Marie Little. Santa Ana: Vision House, 1978.

MacDonald, Gail and Gordon. *If Those Who Reach Could Touch.* Chicago: Moody Press, 1984.
McMinn, Gordon. *Choosing to Be Close: Fill Your Life with Rewarding Relationships.* With Larry Libby. Portland: Multnomah Press, 1984.
Moore, John, and Neff, Ken. *A New Testament Blueprint for the Church.* Foreword by Howard G. Hendricks. Chicago: Moody Press, 1985.
Nystrom, Carolyn. *What Is a Church?* Illustrated by Wayne A. Hanna. Children's Bible Basics. Chicago: Moody Press, 1981.
Smith, David W. *The Friendless American Male.* Foreword by Jim Conway. Ventura: Regal Books, 1983.
Stedman, Ray C. *Body Life.* Glendale: Regal Books, 1972.
Stevens, R. Paul. *Liberating the Laity: Equipping All the Saints for Ministry.* Foreword by Carl Armerding. Downers Grove: InterVarsity Press, 1985.
Swindoll, Charles R. *Dropping Your Guard: The Value of Open Relationships.* Waco: Word Books, 1983.
Swindoll, Charles R. *Improving Your Serve: The Art of Unselfish Living.* Waco: Word Books, 1981.
White, Jerry and Mary. *Friends and Friendship: The Secrets of Drawing Closer.* Colorado Springs: NavPress, 1982.
Williams, June A. *Strategy of Service.* Ministry Resources Library. Grand Rapids: Zondervan Publishing House, 1984.
Wilson, Earl D. *Loving Enough to Care.* Portland: Multnomah Press, 1984.

III. Relating to the Rebels of Love.

Aldrich, Joseph C. *Life-style Evangelism: Crossing Traditional Boundaries to Reach the Unbelieving World.* Portland: Multnomah Press, 1981.
Bjornstad, James. *Counterfeits at Your Door.* Ventura: Regal Books, 1979.
Claerbaut, David. *Urban Ministry.* Foreword by Raymond J. Bakke. Academie Books. Grand Rapids: Zondervan Publishing House, 1983.
Cocoris, G. Michael. *Evangelism: A Biblical Approach.* Foreword by Haddon Robinson. Chicago: Moody Press, 1984.
Coggins, Wade T., and Frizen, Edwin L., Jr., editors. *Reaching Our Generation.* Pasadena: William Carey Library, 1982.
Conn, Harvie M. *Evangelism: Doing Justice and Preaching Grace.* Grand Rapids: Zondervan Publishing House, 1982.
DeMoss, Ted, and Tamasay, Robert. *The Gospel and the Briefcase.* Wheaton: Tyndale House Publishers, Inc., 1984.
Dretke, James P. *A Christian Approach to Muslims: Reflections from West Africa.* Pasadena: William Carey Library, 1979.
Eims, LeRoy. *Laboring in the Harvest.* Colorado Springs: NavPress, 1985.
Geisler, Norman L., and Watkins, William D. *Perspectives: Understanding and Evaluating Today's World Views.* San Bernardino: Here's Life Publishers, Inc., 1984.
Goldberg, Louis. *Our Jewish Friends.* Revised edition. Neptune: Loizeaux Brothers, Inc., 1983.
Hendricks, Howard G. *Say It with Love.* Wheaton: Victor Books, 1972.
Hesselgrave, David J. *Communicating Christ Cross-culturally.* Foreword by Kenneth S. Kantzer. Academie Books. Grand Rapids: Zondervan Publishing House, 1978.

Lau, Lawson. *The World at Your Doorstep: A Handbook for International Student Ministry.* Downers Grove: InterVarsity Press, 1984.
Lum, Ada. *A Hitchhiker's Guide to Missions.* Downers Grove: InterVarsity Press, 1984.
Martin, Walter R. *The Kingdom of the Cults.* Revised edition. Minneapolis: Bethany House Publishers, 1985.
Mayers, Marvin K. *Christianity Confronts Culture: A Strategy for Cross-cultural Evangelism.* Contemporary Evangelical Perspectives. Grand Rapids: Zondervan Publishing House, 1974.
Passantino, Robert and Gretchen. *Answers to the Cultist at Your Door.* Foreword by Walter Martin. Eugene: Harvest House Publishers, 1981.
Peace, Richard. *Small Group Evangelism: A Training Program for Reaching Out with the Gospel.* Downers Grove: InterVarsity Press, 1985.
Petersen, Jim. *Evangelism as a Lifestyle.* Colorado Springs: NavPress, 1980.
Posterski, Don. *Why Am I Afraid to Tell You I'm a Christian? Witnessing Jesus' Way.* Downers Grove: InterVarsity Press, 1983.
Reisinger, Ernest C. *Today's Evangelism: Its Message and Methods.* Phillipsburg: Craig Press, 1982.
Rockwell, Margaret. *Stepping Out: Sharing Christ in Everyday Circumstances.* San Bernardino: Here's Life Publishers, 1984.
Wagner, C. Peter. *On the Crest of the Wave: Becoming a World Christian.* Ventura: Regal Books, 1983.
Wakatama, Pius. *Independence for the Third World Church: An African's Perspective on Missionary Work.* Downers Grove: InterVarsity Press, 1976.